GIRLS, UNLIMITED

Also by Monique Couvson

Too Beautiful for Words

Black Stats: African Americans by the Numbers in the Twenty-first Century

Sing a Rhythm, Dance a Blues: Education for the Liberation of Black and Brown Girls

Cultivating Joyful Learning Spaces for Black Girls: Insights into Interrupting School Pushout

Pushout: The Criminalization of Black Girls in Schools

Charisma's Turn: A Graphic Novel

GIRLS, UNLIMITED

HOW TO INVEST IN OUR DAUGHTERS WITH MORE THAN MONEY

Monique Couvson

NEW YORK
LONDON

Published in the United States by The New Press, New York, 2025
Distributed by Two Rivers Distribution

ISBN 978-1-62079-947-1 (hc)
ISBN 979-8-89385-000-0 (ebook)
CIP data is available

The New Press publishes books that promote and enrich public discussion and understanding of the issues vital to our democracy and to a more equitable world. These books are made possible by the enthusiasm of our readers; the support of a committed group of donors, large and small; the collaboration of our many partners in the independent media and the not-for-profit sector; booksellers, who often hand-sell New Press books; librarians; and above all by our authors.

www.thenewpress.org

Composition by Dix Digital Prepress and Design
This book was set in Garamond Premier Pro

Printed in the United States of America

10 9 8 7 6 5 4 3 2 1

For Allison Ranelle Brown (1976–2020)
And all of our daughters

We will never have to be other than who we are in order to be successful. We realize that we are, ourselves, unlimited, and our experiences valid. It is for the rest of the world to recognize this, if they choose.

—Alice Walker

CONTENTS

INTRODUCTION

Girls are the yolk.

—Nikki Giovanni

I studied her face like I'd studied her poems. Sitting across from me was renowned author, educator, and poet Nikki Giovanni—whom I call Dr. Nikki—and I was thrilled. In 2022, I invited her to have a conversation with me about why society should invest in girls.[1] My vision was inspired by the intergenerational conversation she once shared with the cultural essayist James Baldwin on live TV in 1971, where a then twenty-eight-year-old Nikki Giovanni pressed Baldwin, her elder by nearly twenty years, on a host of issues regarding the conditions in, and collective mindset of, Black America.

After watching that interview many times, I understood the value of intergenerational conversations recorded for viewing decades later, and I wanted to re-create the experience. Dr. Nikki had been my favorite poet since the mid-1980s, when I discovered her work. For decades, I admired her fiery spirit and powerful words. I loved that she always advocated for youth—even tattooing "THUG LIFE" on her forearm as a nod to the infamous tattoo that rapper Tupac Shakur had inked onto his stomach in the 1990s. As he expressed then, THUG LIFE was an acronym for "The Hate U Give Little Infants Fucks Everybody."

The phrase was a critique of the structural and personal violence youth experienced, which negatively impacted society as a whole. When Tupac was killed in 1996, Dr. Nikki got the tattoo to let Tupac's mother, former Black Panther Afeni Shakur, know that her pain was shared.

"I knew it was a sad thing to lose your child," Nikki once told an interviewer. "I just wanted her to know she wasn't alone."[2]

I loved that an elder could "see" us—Generation X and our parents—so clearly and go so far as to replicate our art as protest. In one gesture—replicating Tupac's tattoo—she not only let Tupac's mother know that others were mourning with her but also amplified Tupac's critique. It cemented a special place in my heart for her.

As we sat across from each other, I looked at her petite face, adorned with freckles and beauty marks on her cheeks and around her eyes. They revealed the passing of time, even while her eyes bounced with the same curiosity and challenge on full display in the videos recorded in her youth. As she slowly shifted in her chair, her small emerald studs sparkled under the lights. Her demeanor was relatively reserved: she listened intently to me when I spoke, nodding in agreement or shaking her head with disagreement or clarification at different points in our conversation. She had just turned eighty years old, and I was fifty, so we both had some distance from the youth we had come together to discuss. The intention was not for us to presume consummate knowledge of the current plight of youth but for us to discuss how we, as adults, could support our girls. We had spent more than ninety minutes together, talking about how stories are passed between generations, a discussion that included laughing and teasing each other about the foods we'd prepare and eat as African Americans. We talked about the importance of libraries and the story of Little Red Riding Hood as a metaphor for girls' finding place in society and the value of grandmothers as peacekeepers. She mused about her love for astronomy, what she called "the stars," and the power—or irrelevance—of one's name or racial identity on Earth. According to her, beings in other worlds would just call us "Earthlings," so there is no point in harming people or alienating ourselves because of difference.

When it was time for our conversation to end, I asked, "What can you leave us with on this idea of investment and investing in girls? Why do you think that's important?"

She tilted her head and took a breath. The glasses she had placed on the top of her head clung securely to her soft, curly Afro.

She stared into my eyes and with authority said, "Well, girls are the yolk . . . and I'm not against the white, because the white is there for just one reason: to protect the yolk. And so, if you're a yolk, you have a reason to expect that the white is there to look after you. And your job, then, is to do whatever the dream is, whatever it is that you're doing."[3]

Her analogy of adults as the albumen that protects an egg yolk was powerful to me, and a useful metaphor for how adults should approach working with girls. She placed girls at the center by referring to them as "the yolk," the delicate core of an egg. But more than a clever play on words—especially since girls are born with their lifetime supply of eggs—it was an affirmation that children born biologically female have all they will need to host the reproduction of all human life. While the physical ability to host and grow human life is not the only measure of what makes a child a "girl," I found her invitation compelling. As the albumen, adults have one job: protect them. Nourish them. Ensure that girls have the room to grow.

It was a complex idea presented with great simplicity. Girls are the yolk. If we protect their ability to realize the potential they were born with, we sustain their ability to birth futures that impact all of us.

* * *

Since 1987, I have been an author, an educational advocate, an educator, a researcher, a public intellectual, a filmmaker, an artist, a philanthropist, and, most important, a mother. Specifically, I began my educational advocacy when I was fifteen years old. As a high school student in San Francisco, I immersed myself in an educator-preparation program. Throughout high school and college, I honed my pedagogical practices and research skills, and produced scholarship and programming that explored the unique policies and practices impacting the well-being of Black communities and youth. By the mid-1990s, in graduate school I was keenly aware of the reach of the criminal legal system and began to more deeply explore the conditions of systems-involved young people—youth under the age of eighteen who were impacted by the juvenile court and child welfare systems. My research grew to include advocacy and a deep commitment to articulate the conditions impacting young people. That commitment included sharing the stories of young people who were disproportionately harmed by institutions and beliefs in our society so that they could be seen as more than just "numbers." As an educator, researcher, and author, I was able to function as a translator of sorts, as a trusted purveyor of information between worlds that touch, but that rarely communicate effectively. This is a responsibility that I have taken seriously, and one that I share throughout this book, as it informs my worldview, my advocacy, and my leadership. Each experience has produced its own lessons about the unique conditions of girls. These lessons inform my understanding of what it will take to robustly invest in our girls and their unlimited potential.

My lens is shaped by several critical understandings that inform my ongoing commitment to our girls. The first critical understanding is the importance of *intersectionality* in exploring and discussing the conditions of our girls. Intersectionality is a term coined by legal scholar Kimberlé Crenshaw in 1989 to describe how the combination of each person's identities—including their race, gender, sexuality, class, ability, and so on—inform all of their interactions with people, institutions, and policies.[4] This concept acknowledges that no one ever has only one identity. It acknowledges the laws, protections, and other ways that institutions interact with us at the intersection of our multiple identities. Early on in my own life, I understood that I was both African American and female, which informed how I was experiencing the world around me. When it comes to naming the specific harms that impact our girls and developing the remedies, intersectionality is a critical tool. *Misogynoir,* the term scholar Moya Bailey coined in 2008 to capture the intersections between race and gender that subject Black women to a unique type of hatred, vitriol, and prejudice, is a perfect example of why an intersectional lens is so essential when determining how to robustly invest in our girls.[5] My experiences with and study of misogynoir inform my best thinking about how to invest in our girls in ways that don't simply provide them with strategies to survive dangerous futures.

As president of G4GC, one of the nation's leading philanthropic intermediary organizations focused on resourcing organizations and movements that center the wisdom and well-being of girls and gender-expansive youth of color,* I have worked with an incredible team of advocates, philanthropists, and other co-investors in the well-being of girls to frame the second critical

* A philanthropic intermediary organization functions to connect donors (foundations, individuals, and corporations) with organizations and movements that receive these funds. Intermediaries may regrant funds and provide other supports in alignment with their mission. G4GC's mission is to support transformative organizing work in the United States and territories (Washington, D.C., Puerto Rico, and Guam) centered on an infrastructure that reflects our values, a culture of partnership, healing, reciprocity, and love.

understanding that informs this book: our goal must be the *liberated futures* of our girls.[6] Liberation requires freedom from conditions of harm. Therefore, a liberated future for our girls is a future that is unobstructed, allowing them freedom in thought and behavior. It is the deliberate and intentional act of cultivating futures for our girls in which they are able to actualize their dreams *because* of the significant investments we make. Girls' futures should be informed by love and our commitment to build structural, social, emotional, and community infrastructures that explicitly consider and support them. Their futures shouldn't hinge on their extraordinary resilience under oppression.

In this book, informed by my personal reflections and experiences, I share recommendations for how we can invest in girls to actualize their liberated futures. I also share data and conversations that illustrate how we, as a society, can collectively "protect the yolk." This effort is like jazz—an improvisational, yet syncopated tone to my personal narrative in a call to action. It includes stories from my life and interviews with many of my friends and colleagues, women—some high-profile, some relatively unknown to many—who have shaped much of the contemporary political environment to support the well-being of girls. Overall, this is an invitation to adults to invest by "looking after" girls in a host of measurable and tangible ways. Most people hear the word "investment" and immediately think of financial investments—and that's important. But financial resources are *only one* way that we can secure liberated futures with and for our girls at the intersection of their identities; they are but one strategy to ensure our girls' potential is unlimited.

Starting with the concept of *knowing,* I affirm why it's important for girls. As adults who work with girls, it is important to explore their multiple ways of knowing—and to explore the impacts of these extended epistemologies (the study of how we know what we know)—in our collective work to invest in their well-being. I start here because it's essential to start investing in girls by teaching them the value of their voices and their unique, intuitive understandings. I share insights from interacting with my daughter and talk to my friend sociologist and Episcopalian deacon Bertice Berry about how to recognize *knowing* as an opportunity for investment.

I move on to discuss the importance of supporting girls' purpose once that *knowing* is in place. Once girls know, they *know,* and we cannot take that from them. Our minds and how we spend our time are two of our biggest assets as human beings. Adults are charged with helping girls find their purpose. I share how I discovered my purpose, and how it was supported in the early stages of my life and career.

Next comes an exploration of the structural barriers to girls' success, how to dismantle them, and how to teach girls to have a structural analysis about the world around them. I include excerpts from a conversation with Joanne N. Smith, the CEO of the groundbreaking nonprofit organization Girls for Gender Equity, in which we discuss the development of a national policy agenda for girls and how girls' understanding of policy shapes their ability to actively participate in this democracy. We also discuss a strategy for those who work with girls to ensure that the girls are able to offer more than symbolic presence or tokenism for "youth perspectives."

Next, I explore why protecting girls from gender-based violence is an essential investment in cultivating their ability to realize their purpose and dismantle structural barriers. I share my personal experiences in research and advocacy for girls in this arena, and I include excerpts from a conversation with Tarana Burke, founder of the #metoo movement on why treating gender-based violence as a public health issue is an important investment in girls' liberated futures.

Then I discuss how education and mentorship are essential

investments in girls, reflecting on the key lessons from my work to end school pushout for girls and how my own experiences with mentorship inform my core beliefs about mentorship and education. I discuss how girls are shaping our understanding of educational issues, as well as how investing in girls' education and mentorship is a critical lever for personal growth and their ability to advocate for social policy improvements across a spectrum of issues. I include reflections on how I was mentored, along with notes from two of my own mentees. These are meant to offer transparency about how mentorship has shaped me and how we, as adults, should intentionally mentor girls and young women.

Finally, I acknowledge that while the nonfinancial investments are important, money still matters. This section describes my work at G4GC, and how we were able to build an infrastructure to support more than four hundred girls-serving organizations in their efforts to build liberated futures for girls at the intersection of their identities. This section also explores how money is moving—or not—to girls in ways that are transformative. It outlines how we can include girls in decision-making within philanthropy and across the culture of charitable giving in ways that reflect our belief in the promise of our girls.

Ultimately, this book is a call for adults to use their greatest gifts—their time and their minds—toward the liberation of *all* girls. Framing investments only in financial terms places the onus of "investing" solely in the hands of those with an abundance of financial resources, when the truth is that investing in our girls is the work of more than just the wealthy.

Investing in girls is not about taking resources away from so-called primary issues. My approach to producing research and other scholarship, teaching, advocacy, and philanthropy—which I describe in the chapters that follow—has always been about ensuring we are reaching *all* children in an inherently and defiantly patriarchal social structure. Because ours is a patriarchal society, the measures of success will almost always default to those that involve and impact men and boys. But our efforts to support girls do not require us to take resources aways from boys or anyone else. It's about recognizing the value of a population and its very centrality to the issues we describe as "important." Girls' issues are not stand-alone issues. They are not subsidiary or auxiliary. They are primary. Girls' issues are economic issues. Girls' issues are public health issues. Girls' issues are educational issues. Girls' issues are climate justice issues. Girls' issues are democracy issues.

Every issue is a girls' issue.

1

KNOWING IS GIRLS' SUPERPOWER

I have the nerve to walk my own way, however hard, in my search for reality, rather than climb upon the rattling wagon of wishful illusions.

—Zora Neale Hurston, pioneering Black feminist author and cultural anthropologist

My younger daughter, Mahogany, has always been precocious. For as long as I can remember, she has been inspired by learning and excited to share her knowledge with others. One of my favorite images of her is a photo taken during her third-grade science class in 2012. It shows her reaching upward, rising from her seat as her hand is thrust like a blade above her classmate's head. With a pencil in her other hand resting next to a worksheet and microscope, her head is turned toward the front of the classroom, undoubtedly facing her teacher, Ms. Elaine. Her long dreadlocs neatly pulled back into two ponytails that fell to her elbows, Mahogany's caramel skin pops against a white tee beneath a black long-sleeve shirt. Her lips slightly parted, she is clearly indicating that she's ready to answer a question. My baby knows the answer—or at least she *believes* she does. Honestly, it doesn't even matter if she was actually called on to answer that question or whether her answer was correct; she was actively participating in *learning.*

Another reason I love this photo is the studious look on her classmate's face as she gripped the edge of a pen with her teeth while looking in the same direction as Mahogany. Not only does this image capture a beautiful moment of girls enthralled in learning, but it reflects the incredible work of their teacher to create an environment where girls felt comfortable *engaging.* In classrooms across the U.S., boys dominate in class participation, which is associated with the gender gap in the sciences. By age six, girls believe they are less likely than boys to be "really, really smart."[1] But this photo inspires me to envision a different scenario.

That year, with the encouragement of this same third-grade teacher, my daughter discovered books that developed a voracious appetite for reading in her. By this time, Mahogany and my elder daughter, Ebony, had been traveling with me for years to work events, and they were familiar with my interpretations and articulations of justice. My participatory worldview was familiar to them, as they'd listened to hours of lectures and presentations on race, gender, justice, and education. They understood my fundamental commitment to the idea that people at the center of any inquiry should be involved in the collection and interpretation of any data such an inquiry yields. They knew that my critique of social and systemic patriarchy—how social institutions are often structured to reify the presumptive supremacy of men—was an extension of my belief in equity, in my belief that all people should have equal access to a life of dignity and respect. In their earlier years, they toddled around my office as I led research on the prevalence and impact of racial and gender discrimination in the public sector, and they took pride in dressing professionally to march around my office at the NAACP National Headquarters. They both learned about social responsibility—the notion that they would use their talents and skills to contribute positively to society—early and knew that they would have the freedom to pursue their own paths toward becoming the best version of themselves—with one requirement. I asked that *whatever* they do, they do it toward the advancement of freedom, for themselves, and for their people. They agreed, understanding early that as African Americans, we are the descendants of people who survived one of the most heinous and egregious efforts in history to dehumanize and subjugate our ancestors. They have also demonstrated their understanding by embracing their freedom to pursue whatever field of endeavor that appeals to them. Naturally inquisitive and lacking the filter that typically comes with age and discernment, Mahogany liked to ask a lot of questions. She had specific questions about freedom; so she started to answer them for herself in the third grade by reading the narratives of enslaved people. I noticed that this interest in justice led her to pay close attention when I was lecturing or talking to colleagues about strategies for freedom to take shape.

For example, in the early 2010s, I had written a report for the African American Policy Forum, a national think tank led by prominent legal scholar Kimberlé Crenshaw, which brings together "academics, activists, and policymakers" in an interdisciplinary interrogation of how to dismantle structure inequality.[2] My report, titled "Race, Gender, and School to Prison Pipeline," was about expanding the "school-to-prison pipeline" to include an analysis for Black girls. In it, I explored how existing frameworks and data captured (or failed to capture) the specific experiences of girls along the continuum of experiences associated with the use of discipline in schools.[3] Following the release of that paper, I met with Kimberlé Crenshaw and another impressive legal scholar, Priscilla Ocen, to discuss how we could continue to amplify the need for social, institutional, and economic investments to improve the plight of Black girls. We decided to meet in Monterey, California. A coastal town known for its beaches, a world-class aquarium, and proximity to blue whales of the Pacific Ocean, Monterey was a perfect location between

Oakland, where I was based at the time, and Los Angeles, where they were. We spent our time together exploring how we might begin to make academic concepts relatable to the public, and how we might continue to amplify the voices of girls in ongoing public discourses about educational equity. We talked through potential approaches to popularize rhetoric that includes women and girls in narratives about the impact of racial bias. And, as I had done over the course of their lives, I brought my daughters to work with me.

After a full day of meeting, we broke for dinner. Both girls were excited to finally get outside to the boardwalk, so they quickly assembled by the door as we prepared to leave the hotel. Mahogany walked up to Priscilla and asked a question not uncommon for inquisitive and unfiltered children.

"How old are you?" she asked.

"How old do you think I am?" Priscilla responded.

Mahogany looked at her carefully and then replied, "Nineteen."

Priscilla laughed and pulled Mahogany in close. "See," she chuckled. "I love you."

Mahogany smiled, satisfied by the affirmation, and went on to tell Priscilla more about herself. After a short conversation about the gracious aging process for Black women—how "Black don't crack"—I looked on as Mahogany continued her conversation with Priscilla.

"I've read so many books," she announced, beaming with pride.

"That's great," Priscilla said in a soft and even tone. "But what's really important is that you have a *critical analysis."*

"Critical analysis?" Mahogany repeated, her eight-year-old voice softening with uncertainty.

"Critical analysis," Pricilla repeated firmly.

Mahogany nodded—and she's been nurturing this notion in her expressions of leadership ever since. As her mother, I remain grateful to Priscilla for sharing that nugget of wisdom and truth with my daughter. Both of my daughters have had the opportunity to interface with many powerhouse women throughout their lives, and this is among my favorite moments, because in that exchange, Priscilla challenged Mahogany to do more than just read. She wanted her to *think*. She encouraged her to *know*. She wanted her to *lead* with this knowing. And this underscored the importance for me to continue teaching both of my daughters the power of engaging each and every way we might acquire and express knowledge. *Activating the critical analysis of girls unlocks their ability to access their multiple ways of knowing.*

These early conversations with Priscilla and others throughout her adolescence provided a foundation for Mahogany to take control of her learning journey. They allowed her to move forward at the speed of her intentions and interest, to activate her intelligence when and how she chose to. The confidence of knowing how to control her learning journey set her on a path that would ultimately lead her to her finish college early and begin graduate school at the age of twenty-one. She was able to do this while maintaining her commitment to her community. She studied to become a doula at the age of sixteen during the global COVID-19 pandemic so that she might become a more effective advocate for teen mothers. In a time of extraordinary exposure to death, I watched her choose life. A couple of years later, she launched a zine* entitled *Revolutionary Dreaming* to ensure that the cultural contributions of Black girls in literary spaces were documented and amplified. Named in tribute to the poem by renowned poet Nikki Giovanni, *Revolutionary Dreaming* is "a zine for Black girl literary artists, and is edited, illustrated, and organized by young

* A zine—short for "fanzine"—is an independent publication that circulates to fewer than 1,000 people. Zines may take many forms. *Revolutionary Dreaming* is primarily shared online, with a limited number of print editions available for distribution.

Black women under the age of 24."[4] It publishes poetry, flash fiction, short plays, short screenplays, and nonfictional essays that are "inspired by the intellectual artistry of our Black literary foremothers," as "a living archive of, for, and by Black girl writers, essayists, and storytellers."[5] Mahogany, who also serves as editor in chief for the zine, has grown through her literary art, her study, her volunteer work, and her intensive engagement with programs such as the community organization Justice for Black Girls, a nonprofit founded by educator Brianna Baker as a "social justice education space that serves Black girls' needs for protection, safety, and belonging through a holistic culture of care coupled with Black feminist curriculum, grassroots collaborations, and academic partnerships."[6] Mahogany has developed a deep understanding of the importance of creating opportunities for girls' voices to be heard. She understands that transferring knowledge in a way that allows girls to recognize the brilliance of their lived experiences facilitates their freedom.

"Some girls don't necessarily have language for liberation," Mahogany said to me one day, reflecting on her volunteer work as a college student mentoring middle school girls in Atlanta. "They haven't developed language yet, or an understanding of what's going on—for the harm that they're experiencing and feeling on a day-to-day basis. So, I think it's best to be gracious with them, planting the seed of possibility in them; and letting them know 'you don't have to rush this.'"

By "this," Mahogany means their own understanding of their experiences and how to communicate their thoughts and feelings about it. Girls are often expected to have an assessment and analysis of their experiences immediately. They're expected to be able to provide perceptive insights at an unreasonable pace that doesn't give them time to figure it out for themselves before having to disclose their vulnerabilities to the world. Mahogany is offering that girls can reject this expectation in favor of a more liberating timeline for their healing—and their communication about that to others. These are the origins of "*knowing*," the practice of embracing a higher consciousness. *Knowing* is the state of understanding that comes after processing information in the mind, body, and spirit. It is a physical and metaphysical experience—and a practice that Mahogany has committed to personally. It is one of the seeds she plants in her peers and other girls. Other girls have recognized Mahogany for being a keeper of stories and creator of a digital home through which Black girls, and anyone who reads their words, can acknowledge the value of their stories and increase understanding of their lives. One day, Mahogany—who was only nineteen years old herself—shared an email she received from an eighteen-year-old who had just been notified that her submission had been accepted for publication in the zine. It read:

> *OH MY GOODNESS!!!!! This is the biggest deal of my life ever!!!! Thank you so much for accepting this piece, it is easily the most important, personal, and healing thing I've ever created for myself. Thank you a million times over for encouraging me to believe in/bet on me!!! Excited to see what comes next. ;-)*

When Mahogany shared this with me, her facial expression was a cross between excitement and awe. The wonder in her eyes revealed that she perhaps hadn't fully realized the value of what she had created until seeing this note from a peer. But I saw it. The zine was an ambitious undertaking for an undergraduate student, but beyond that, it was an audacious expression of a desire to be acknowledged. Girls are often told to "be seen and not heard," and described as "sugar and spice, and everything nice." These were supposed to be tactics to help girls stay out of trouble, and to stay in their place. By creating a literary zine for Black girls, Mahogany was countering this narrative and challenging the "places" where girls belong. Not only are the girls who contribute to her publication seen and heard, they are encouraged to do so with authenticity. This allows them to see themselves and grow in their power.

I remember witnessing this firsthand when the Social Justice Program at Spelman College hosted a reception to celebrate the launch of the inaugural issue of the zine in 2023. The issue, titled *Internal Reparations: What Do Black Girls Owe Themselves?,* announced the arrival of bold Black girls unapologetically centering their imaginations, reflections, and analyses on the topic. I was beyond proud—and honored to attend along with several of the contributors, including eleven-year-old Makena, the issue's youngest contributor. Surrounded by her father and little brother, Makena walked in the room with a quiet confidence that caused us all to notice her. Her box braids cascading down her back, she commanded space in a red Hello Kitty sweater, black skirt, and side-body purse. She was dressed for the occasion, and I loved it.

"We're so proud of you," I said to her. "How do you feel?"

"Well," she said with a shrug, "I've never been a published author before."

Those were shy words, but when she began to read from her original poem, her power was evident.

"Black girls owe themselves the world," she began. She paused, cleared her throat, and continued. "With their beauty and strength unfurled, they owe themselves the right to dream, and the power to make their voices scream. . . ."

I was grateful to bear witness to the unfurling of her strength as an author. Later that night, Makena giggled, snacked, autographed copies of the zine, and posed for selfies—including one with me. She was a testament to why platforms for girls to express themselves are so important. When our girls are seen and heard, they create spaces not only for themselves to flourish but for others in their communities as well.

Mahogany has been one of my greatest examples of why investing in girls' *knowing* is an important first step to securing their well-being. The early exchanges and role modeling in Mahogany's life prepared her to encourage the use of an extended epistemology, or using her multiple ways of knowing, by volunteering to mentor and guide younger girls. When Mahogany claimed space to and for her own voice to emerge, she gave herself permission to be excited about her own learning. It allowed her to recognize in herself the capacity to articulate, determine, and control her own liberated future. Although she had her fair share of growing pains, including having to experience a relatively serious surgery in middle school and managing a contentious divorce between her father and me in high school, no one can take from her the investments that she makes in the sources of her knowing—her mind and her soul.

This chapter began with an example from my daughter's life, but the truth is that this wisdom is ancestral. I was able to recognize and support the development of this critical skill because it was first supported in me. My mother—a single mom from San Francisco—gave birth to me when she was twenty-three years old. In the year I was born, the city was a place where roughly 13 percent of the population was African American—the highest it's ever been.[7] Black bodies were a routine part of the public and social landscape, not the scant presence that they have become. As a home to people of many different racial and ethnic groups, San Francisco was a unique place where people of European, Asian, Indigenous, Latine, and African descent commonly interacted with each other. We learned together. We worked together. We played together. Of course, San Francisco remained, like many other places across the country, rigidly segregated in structure; but as children, we experienced a brief moment in time between the 1970s and 1980s where we were free to explore each other's cultures and engage in exchanges that made us stronger for our proximity to each other. But I wouldn't call it a melting pot. For example, in 1978, the San Francisco branch of the NAACP filed a lawsuit against the San Francisco Unified School District (SFUSD) alleging racial discrimination and persistent racial segregation.[8] Five years later, SFUSD, the State Department of Education, and the San Francisco branch of the NAACP entered a legal settlement known as a Consent Decree, which sought to end the racial segregation of the city's public schools, particularly as it impacted African American students. Several agreements were made as a part of that settlement, including racial "caps"—or quotas to ensure that one racial group would not dominate—in the student composition of schools, including at elite schools that tended to be dominated by one or two racial groups. For nearly three decades, legal challenges to these caps were brought before the court as the demographics of San Francisco's population shifted, ultimately leading to an abandonment of the student placement requirements that momentarily led to more integrated schools in the city. Still, those of us growing up in San Francisco at the time enjoyed a brief period in which children playing in Mission Dolores Park or teenagers skating in Golden Gate Park on Sundays reflected a kind of cultural and racial gumbo.

From the time of my birth, my mother knew that she wanted to support my curiosity and my capacity to learn and acquire information. She taught me to aim high and set extraordinary goals for myself. She encouraged me to meditate and to recognize my brain as my most powerful asset. She would say, "The mind is amenable to suggestion," and demand that I take great caution with what I exposed it to. This meant that I was allowed to watch neither horror movies nor the popular TV show *Good Times,* about a Black family struggling to survive in housing projects, which she saw as equally harmful.

"They never get out of the ghetto," she'd say bluntly.

At the time, I felt robbed of a cultural experience because all of my peers were allowed to watch the shows and films that were prohibited in my household. Only later would I appreciate what my mother was protecting me from: the romanticization of stagnation and fear. She did not want me to get comfortable with even the *idea* of good times if the conditions required marginalization. The power of humor and the show's cultural significance aside, she was protecting me from believing in the inevitability of poverty. She understood that I would believe what I was taught, and would manifest whatever I believed.

"God makes everything possible," she often said to me. "And your mind can do anything you put it to."

When I entered kindergarten, my mother enrolled me in a French American bilingual school. Occasionally, a teacher would catch the same bus as us on our way to school. As I shared conversations with this teacher in French, other passengers—and the bus driver—would look on, curious about the little Black girl who sat alongside her mother, speaking French even though her mother clearly did not. My maternal ancestry hails from the American South, but my mother always held an interest in French language and culture.

When I asked her what inspired her to place me in a French immersion school, she replied simply, "I wanted you to have a leg up."

It was a simple statement, but loaded with an acknowledgment that my life would be met with obstacles to advancement given the body that I was in, so I would need to constantly cultivate a competitive edge in order to thrive. I didn't fully understand it then, but later I learned that she was, indeed, preparing me for success with this important decision to introduce me to a second language at such an early age. Children with exposure to a second language in their early stages of development experience cognitive advantages that monolingual children do not have.[9] Proficiency benefits them academically, and it also increases their capacity to engage an inclusive worldview. These are skills that few American children have access to, let alone African American children.

As a child, I didn't question it; but I remember only two other Black children in the class and a cluster of Chicano, Asian, and other students of color with whom I was also learning French. I just remember registering that I was different from other children at school because I didn't speak French at home; and different from the other children in my neighborhood *because* I spoke French at school. Aware of my unique positioning, my mother commissioned a plaque for me that read: *Si vous ne pouvez pas le faire vous-même, ne me demandez pas de le faire pour vous. Compris*? [English translation: If you cannot do it, don't ask me to do it for you. Understand?]

Some nights, I would stare at the engraved sign and wonder what it meant. At times it felt harsh and isolating—after all, as my only active parent, she was the *only* one I could rely on. If I couldn't go to her for help, where could I go? Then it finally occurred to me that, interpreted for the circumstances of my life, I could not expect to go to her when I had a question from school because it was a language she didn't understand. I couldn't ask her to give me something she did not have. However, while *she* did not speak French and would not be able to help me with my homework or other affairs from school, she asked a trusted co-worker, who was Parisian, to read my report cards and translate them for her. Although I couldn't go to *her* for this type of specific help, she had built a community for me.

I made my way through the bilingual program through third grade, after which the financial cost became too great for me to continue. For the fourth grade, my mother enrolled me in a small parochial school in the Western Edition neighborhood of San Francisco, where my learning journey would continue. Although my formal French immersion education ended abruptly, I was ultimately able to send my daughters to a French bilingual school in the East Bay through to the completion of their written and oral fluency. Blessed to send them to this school even when paying for it was a challenge, I was always clear that learning French (or any second language) was about more than learning to perfectly transcribe a text during *dictée* or being able to shop easily in Paris. Language access is a gateway to freedom. My mom knew it, and so do I.

Language is a tool through which we reflect knowledge, a way to communicate what we are thinking. However, there are multiple ways of knowing and therefore multiple languages to communicate such knowing. Welsh scholar Cen Williams coined the term "translanguaging" in 1994 "to describe pedagogical strategies in bilingual classrooms that did not strictly separate the use of two languages in instruction."[10] However, literacy scholar Brittany Frieson and bilingual education scholar Vivian Presiado offer an effective framework for applying the concept of translanguaging to girls. They offer that girls often engage in "translanguaging" by creating spaces that foster what scholars describe as "extraordinary openness, critical exchange where the geographical image can be expanded to encompass a multiplicity of perspectives . . . a space where issues of race, class, and gender can be addressed simultaneously."[11] Girls' capacity to negotiate language and bend it to serve the full extent of what we know as their "counternarratives" is richly illustrated by a 2021 study on multilingual Black girls. In this study, Presiado and Frieson discuss the cultural, linguistic, and verbal dexterity of two fourth-grade Black girls participating in dual language bilingual education (DLBE). In their work, which "draws attention to the nuanced nature of Black American girls' literacies that are typically ignored in and beyond DBLE spaces," Presiado and Frieson also masterfully present the power harnessed by investing in girls' capacity to communicate their thoughts, feelings, and actions with confidence. In their study on "Black girls' education in multilingual spaces and their beautiful ways of being and knowing," the authors demonstrate how girls mix cultural vernacular and language repertoire with what they call "survival literacies"—an extension of Elaine Richardson's exploration of Black girl literacies that "carve out free spaces in oppressive locations such as the classroom, the streets, or the airwaves."[12] Richardson's work on Black girl literacies provides a framework for recognizing the extended epistemologies practiced by girls, Black girls in particular, who couple presentational knowing—awareness of symbols, story, imagery, for example—with propositional knowing, understanding of the theories and data that allow them to concretely describe the phenomenon or issue they are examining. In doing this, girls can locate not only themselves in a broader conversation or condition, they can identify and practice ways to be safe. This is important, because it signals the expansion of *knowing*—and the way girls creatively express their connection to learning and belonging, no matter where they are. Seeing language as more than spoken word also allows for the exchange of information through nonverbal communication. High school and college girls that I have spoken with across the nation often share stories of knowing when another girl may be in harm's way. These girls recognize the suspicious behavior of a person whose energy feels predatory, or who is exhibiting signs of intended harm (such as following this girl, watching her movements closely, and moving close to her). They speak of signaling to other girls if they witness the behavior or taking precautions such as moving to a different location to keep themselves safe. Language can also open one's capacity to engage with communities and situations *outside* of one's normed experiences. For girls, these skills are critical to advancement in spaces that default to patriarchal frameworks, which inherently facilitate an erasure of their communication skills —verbal and nonverbal.

* * *

The idea that girls should be seen and not heard is not a uniquely American phenomenon. Historically, across the globe, different cultures have embraced this normed idea of gendered behavior. The silencing of girls has fundamentally distorted our collective understanding of, and appreciation for, girls' transformative leadership. To be relegated to silence is a deliberate position that, while meant to stifle voice and participation, can also create conditions for exploration, observation, and analysis. A 2023 Centre for Economic Policy Research study on perceptions of gender norms in sixty countries across North America and five other continents found that while support for women's "basic rights (i.e., freedom to work outside of the home)" is underestimated, especially among men, there is significantly less support for gender-based affirmative action.[13] So, even while the global perception of basic parity between men and women is emergent, the desire to take actions that enforce or correct power imbalances associated with antiquated ideas about the roles of women and girls is low.[14] Patriarchy and anti-youth bias create norms that adultify girls who dare to speak up, and that punish them if what they say critiques the status quo.

Classroom teachers have been found to engage less frequently with girls, as compared with boys, asking them fewer questions in class and spending less time with them as learners, which can consequently make girls less likely to raise their hands in class.[15] Their leadership in schools and other public spaces also become less visible as they progress through school. Nearly one in three Latine girls fear being "embarrassed or ridiculed" for taking on a leadership role in school, according to Girls Leadership, a nonprofit organization in the U.S. that uses social-emotional programming to **teach girls to exercise the power of their voices.**[16] By centering gender and racial equity in their efforts to address the barriers to leadership development for girls, Girls Leadership explores the dynamic nature of why investing in girls' ways of knowing—and its expression through leadership—is essential. If girls believe they can be leaders, they can build the skills to actualize it. If they activate their *knowing* in their understanding and practice of leadership, the reach of their wisdom grows exponentially. Girls do not interpret leadership—or view their participation in it—as a monolith. This is important, because it also means that there is more than one way to invest in their leadership. Black (34 percent) and Latine (29 percent) girls score higher than other girls on the Roets Rating Scale for Leadership—a self-reporting scale that measures ambition and leadership in late elementary school through high school—and they are more likely to identify as leaders. Almost half (48 percent) of Black girls self-identify as leaders, compared to 36 percent of Latine/Hispanic girls, 33 percent of multiethnic girls, 31 percent of white girls, and 25 percent of Asian girls.[17] Labels such as "bossy," "pushy," or racially coded language about girls and young women who activate their voices by speaking up for their well-being, such as "fiery," or "spicy," may discourage these girls from engaging these skills in their homes, schools, or communities. However, when adults encourage these skills and create conditions for girls to safely speak up, the girls reveal how much they aspire to leadership. For example, in their first youth-led research study on Asian American, Native Hawaiian, and Pacific Islander girls and gender-expansive youth, Girls Leadership found that 54 percent of these young people "don't think of themselves as a leader now, but want to be a leader in the future."[18] The study also found that for these young people, being a leader is less about being "in charge of other people and making decisions to affect them," and more about "bringing people together to get things done."[19] As one eighteen- to twenty-two-year-old South Asian, first-generation student said, "Leadership is not just making speeches and portraying yourself as being the right one. I think it's a lot more of how you are supporting your community without overshadowing your community."[20]

* * *

Women have been at the forefront of advocacy for girls to be included in public discourses on their well-being. For example, in response to the gap in philanthropic resources reaching Black girls in the South, cofounder of Black Voters Matter and philanthropist LaTosha Brown founded the Southern Black Girls and Women's Consortium and the Black Girls Dream Fund. Black women and girls receive less than 1 percent of philanthropic giving, and more than half of the Black population in the United States lives in the South. Under Brown's leadership, the fund awarded more than $10 million to more than 220 organizations in thirteen states in the American South, eclipsing previous funding to Black girls in that region.[21]

Women have been effective leaders in corporations, government, nonprofit advocacy organizations, communities, and their own families because of their propensity to engage and integrate a host of perspectives that elevate a collective capacity for greatness. For example, without Lucy Wheelock, an American educator born in 1857 whose avocation for kindergarten education transformed the practice of teaching young children, modern school systems would not be rigorously organized around the notion of starting when students are five years old.[22] Another leader was Patsy Takemoto Mink, the first woman of color elected to Congress in 1964. She was denied opportunities to pursue her academic and professional area of interest (medicine), until she became a policymaker, coauthored Title IX—which mandated equal treatment between males and females in education—and shifted the landscape of opportunity of girls and women in the U.S. I have often talked about girls, particularly girls of color, as critical articulators of the possibility for justice. Just as those closest to the problem are best equipped to develop remedies, those who have been most marginalized have the most insight about society's margins.

Congresswoman Mink once told a reporter, "I didn't start off wanting to be in politics. . . . Not being able to get a job from anybody changed things."[23] Title IX, which Congresswoman Mink coauthored, was part of the 1972 Education Amendments that prohibited discrimination based on sex in schools and other educational programming and activities, and is responsible for leveling the playing field for girls and young women throughout education. Before Title IX was implemented, just 300,000 girls participated in high school sports nationwide; now that number is about 3.4 million.[24] For many women, their experiences as girls become driving forces behind their advocacy as adults, and in their determination to create a landscape of opportunity for girls that is better than the one they experienced. Everyone can—and should—do that.

Refining girls' ways of knowing is mostly about cultivating girls' ability to access resources that help them make informed decisions about their lives and their futures. It is about challenging them to increase the rigor of their analyses so that they are not just absorbing information but thinking *critically* about the information they absorb. Critical thinking is a skill that allows girls to challenge lies that are told about them, and helps them to resist participating in their own oppression by repeating these harmful statements or beliefs.[25] In late February 2024, I visited a leadership group of fifteen high school girls in Long Island, New York, to talk about *Charisma's Turn,* my graphic novel about girls and their gifts. We convened in the school's multipurpose room, where the girls sat around circular tables, quietly jotting notes onto sheets of paper and snacking on fruits and bagels that had been prepared for them. I was the guest speaker, so they all graciously listened to me as I talked with them about my journey from being a researcher to working in philanthropy, and shared tidbits about why focusing on the well-being of girls was important to me.

As I spoke, I took in the sight of each girl's body language and level of engagement. A girl wearing blue scrubs sat toward the front of the classroom, barely taking notes or moving in her seat, but her eyes followed everything I said. Another girl, wearing an off-shoulder top and jeans, periodically tucked her black hair behind her ears and adjusted her top, as her eyes followed my movements in the front of the room. But there was one girl in particular who seemed fixated on my every word. She wore a hoodie and sweats, with long, color-treated Senegalese twists framing her face. She stared at me through her glasses, nodding occasionally, in agreement with something I said. I paused to invite questions, at which point a few hands went up.

"What is the Black Girl Freedom Fund?" one girl asked.

"How can I get an internship?" asked another.

Finally, I called on the girl with the glasses. "When are you going to write your story?" she asked.

It was a mature question, and seemingly unprovoked. We were there to discuss girls' leadership. However, I had just talked to them about how I got to where I was professionally, and she wanted to know more. Her critical thinking skills allowed her to not only question what was presented to her; they were also inviting her to consider what she *wanted.* In many ways, her question conjured this book.

Adults of all genders should care about girls' well-being not only if they are partnered with a male or will give birth to someone identified as male. When poet and feminist essayist Audre Lorde correctly identified that women could be "dangerous" to structures of oppression, she was inviting women and girls to hone our ability to articulate our visions for the future. Our clear visions for the future can disrupt those structures of oppression. When she warned, *"your silence will not protect you,"* I believe she was also imploring us to examine the power of women's and girls' voices and to find ways to reject the weaponization of our silence. It's not just that being silent is a problem. It's that girls' silence is often misinterpreted—or intentionally misread—by the adults in their lives because society, informed by its racial and gender biases, is committed to a lack of fluency in interpreting silence. As thirteenth-century poet and Islamic scholar Rumi put it, "I closed my mouth and spoke to you in a hundred silent ways."

Knowing the difference between silence and complacency—and teaching our daughters the difference—is an important element in preparing them to challenge the forces that may seek to conflate the two. While complacency is inaction that creates room for harmful activities to grow—because of a real or perceived agreement with those actions—silence can also be quite active. For example, I have experienced girls who sit quietly, but their eyes and body language signal a very active engagement with what is being shared with them—either through facial cues such as pursed lips or raised eyebrows, or by furiously scribbling notes, typing into their phones or computers, or drawing pictures that signal that their minds are processing the material. Silence can signal dissent, too, as in 2011, when I witnessed a group of college-aged young women in Northern California refuse to ask any questions of a guest lecturer who had insulted women and girls by insinuating that families needed to revolve around the well-being of men and boys. It can also signal contemplation, such as when a girl was asked during a virtual meeting in 2022 about how young people would want to steward resources if they had the opportunity to do so.

"If you could invest $10,000 today, where would you put it?" I asked.

She looked into the camera and said nothing. I smiled and waited patiently.

Another participant in the meeting jumped in, slightly uncomfortable with the silence. She attempted to rephrase the question, when the first girl stopped her.

"No," she said. "I understand . . . this is just my *opportunity.* I want to make sure I take my time."

Her silence marked her thinking about how she wanted to respond, how she could take advantage of the "opportunity" before her by giving an answer worthy of the question. It was, in itself, a response and a reflection of her understanding of why it was better to be quiet in that moment, rather than blurt out something that did not reflect her understanding of the opportunity at hand.

If we "read" silence, then we seek to understand the space it leaves in our consciousness to reach new ways of being—or of creating new spaces for emergent conversations. For girls, there is often a risk associated with speaking out. Sometimes girls are reprimanded for speaking their minds—they are seen as too "sassy" or "bossy" when they assert themselves. According to University of Pennsylvania Wharton School of Business professor Adam Grant, the social hierarchy as informed by power and status determines whether or not girls will be called "bossy" for asserting leadership. He wrote, "When young women get called bossy, it's often because they're trying to exercise power without status. It's not a problem that they're being dominant; the backlash arises because they're 'overstepping' their perceived status."[26] But it's precisely this risk we need more girls to take. As former Facebook COO Sheryl Sandberg once said, "That girl's not bossy. She has executive leadership skills."[27] Teaching girls how to discern is important for their physical and emotional safety. Teaching girls when to own their learning process at every stage of their development leads them on the path toward being unlimited.

In late 2016, I was on a book tour for *PUSHOUT* and visited a small, rural college of under five thousand undergraduate students in the Northeast. Donald Trump had just been elected the forty-fifth president of the United States, igniting a wave of intentionally abusive speech and behavior among young men across the country. When I arrived in town, one of the professors who had invited me picked me up from the airport. As we drove to campus, I asked her if there was anything I should know before I launched into my lecture that evening. Whenever I travel and speak to a new audience, I always ask this question to help root me in the place where I am visiting, to give me some perspective of the climate on campus. At first she hesitated. Then, after some prodding on my end, she shared that there was a group of White male students who were following African American women on campus, chanting "Trump! Trump!" behind them as an intimidation tactic. From what I understood, those young women did not fall for the bait by escalating the situation, but rather used their sense of *knowing* to get themselves to safety and engage the faculty—and security—as appropriate. Immediately, I felt empathy for these female students. I could imagine how vulnerable—and angry—they must have felt . . . even as they were outnumbered by the pack of male students shouting at them. As appalling as this situation was, I wasn't completely surprised. Trump's own reckless language about sexual assault and acts of physical intimidation of women (including his practice of standing over Hillary Clinton to intimidate her during a presidential debate) had revived and endorsed a toxic social environment antithetical to inclusion and respect for women.

As I was approaching the hall where I was to deliver my lecture, I noticed that there were several male students wearing shirts that read "All Lives Matter," and a few of those faces looked at me with a palpable disdain. I have come to trust my instincts, as an extension of my experiential *knowing,* and I can certainly tell when someone's energy is dangerous or unsettling, so I took note. As the Black Lives Matter movement was taking off in 2013, many public figures and vocal dissenters to the virtues of pluralism misinterpreted—or distorted—the slogan to suggest that "only" Black lives matter, which is neither stated nor implied. It was a contentious subject through the 2010s, and left many—including myself—wondering why it was so difficult for some people to understand that people of African descent were responding to the specific anti-Blackness that threatened our lives.[28] After registering where the "All Lives Matter" folks were, I continued my way into the room.

Once at the podium, I surveyed the crowd. I said a silent prayer and honored the intuition—the *knowing* in my body—that was telling me to move forward, to give my lecture as planned. I looked into the sea of faces, which was a spectacular reflection of a variety of racial and ethnic backgrounds packed into a large conference area, and then decided to prepare a request for our collective well-being.

"Tonight, we are going to talk about race, gender, and the criminalization of Black girls," I said. "As this is a place of learning, I would like to invite us all to approach this conversation with an open mind and a degree of safety."

I noticed waves of head nodding among the audience. This signaled to me that there was an appreciation for what I was asking, and a general sentiment of agreement.

"I ask us to be in agreement that we can uphold that safety for this conversation," I continued. "If you agree, please say 'yes.'"

"Yes!" the crowd roared in unison.

I let out a sigh. Honestly, I was relieved that the room was filled with people who were genuinely interested in learning and talking through the issues I came to present. But there was still some unfinished business needed to secure the safety of the space.

"If you do *not* agree or if you don't think you can help uphold the safety of this space, please feel free to leave at this time. No judgment," I said.

I stepped back from the podium and scanned the crowd. A few of the people whose energy I had noticed earlier got up and walked out of the room. It was the only time that I have ever done something like that, but I had learned to lean into the multiple ways that I can sense safety, and I knew that space wasn't safe. I guess these individuals saw that they were outnumbered and decided to leave us to our business that night. I prayed quickly and silently that they would not return with weapons; then I took a deep breath and again approached the podium.

"All right," I said. "Let's get to work."

It was a scary moment—though just one of many nights I would find myself traipsing across the country, inviting people to explore their biases against Black girls. I traveled alone for most of those trips, which some of my colleagues and staff believed to be dangerous. Frequently during these trips, random mothers and community elders that I had just met that evening would lay hands on and pray over me, pleading for my Divine protection. Other towns made sure to have ample representation from members of my public service sorority in the crowd, so that I was never truly "alone." Doing the work of researching, writing, and then educating the public about the specific conditions that negatively impact Black girls is addressing both racial and gender biases simultaneously—and it can be nerve-racking at times, especially when I have to make split-second decisions about how to control a potentially volatile situation. But stillness, faith, and focus on my purpose have never failed me. These are cornerstones of my *knowing,* and the praxis for my leadership.

Nearly ten years later, I was talking to my friend Bertice Berry about that incident, still grateful and marveling at the fact that those individuals left and did not return with an intent to commit harm. Bertice is most well known as a prominent sociologist who was one of the first scholars to have her own syndicated talk show in the 1990s, *The Bertice Berry Show.* Her scholarship, lectures, and training center on leadership development and internal wellness. In 2024, she was ordained as a deacon in the Episcopal Church, anchoring her more firmly in her faith, and in her call to connect the world with the church.

"Can you believe that happened to me?" I asked.

"Yeah, I believe you, because I was with some others at a

Harris-Walz* rally in Savannah in 2024 and it was clear that these people were planning to disrupt . . . and some of them did. But somebody laid hands on them and prayed them out. That prayer got those people out of an arena of about ten thousand people."

We agreed that this was an example of how we, as women—once girls—activated this intuition, this sense of *knowing*. She went on to share her theory of how girls come to develop this sense of knowing and why it often develops from challenging circumstances.

"I think there are girls in what I call 'the cracks.' Sometimes the cracks are race. Sometimes the cracks are *race and* class. The cracks are *always* gender. The girls who are the most shut out from society, they're the ones who have the deepest sense of *knowing*—at a spiritual level, at an intuitive level, at an intellectual level. But we—adults and society at large—ignore them. We miss the very folks that we need, not just in conversations between you and me, but that society needs in every room. Instead of being *safe*, we need to create spaces for girls that are *loving*, because a safe space isn't always loving, but a loving space is always safe."

I agreed, enthusiastically.

"A person who falls between those cracks is the one, the very one decision-makers need," Bertice continued.

I nodded, fully absorbing that the girls whom society fails are the ones we should be looking out for, and learning from.

"Nobody knew that I wanted to go to college until one of my high school teachers said to me, you should go to college," she continued. "But every time they had an altar call at church for the unspoken requests,† I was praying for my mother to get

* "Harris-Walz" refers to the 2024 Democratic presidential ticket, where Kamala Harris was campaigning for president of the United States and Timothy Walz was campaigning for vice president.

† An altar call is a practice common in the Christian faith when the pastor or preacher asks members and attendees in the sanctuary to join them at

saved and for me to go to college. I never uttered it out loud. Because as a child, you just *know*. For instance, I knew what to say to the cleaning women when I was just a 'cleaning girl.' I knew those old women who got on the same bus as me had to know more than I knew about cleaning houses, and I wanted to stand out. They saw me as a kid. I was twelve or thirteen years old . . ."

I sat up in my seat. I, too, used to clean homes as a domestic worker from a young age.

"I was a cleaning girl at twelve, too, to help cover a family debt," I said. "I used to have to clean a German lady's house. One of my early moments of *knowing* was when I was cleaning her floor, scrubbing the baseboards, and she walked in with her family. Referring to me, she said, 'Oh, that's my girl,' then walked past me without looking. I felt like a slave, because of the way she said it. It was as if she owned me. And her grandchild, who was about my age, looked at me on my knees and then looked away. I remember thinking, *Oh, this is* not *it*."

"Right!" Bertice said, agreeing.

"The woman I worked for flicked her wrist at me, in an exaggerated gesture to turn off the television, because she didn't want me to watch it. Her kids were watching a cartoon on Saturday morning as I was walking by with a bucket, slowly. Of course I wanted to watch what they were watching. But the woman says, 'You're here to clean' and smacks the button of the television to turn it off. Then she told her kids to watch television in the den. Her little boy turned around and mouthed 'I'm sorry' to me."

"He knew," she continued. "He *knew*."

Bertice marinated in her recognition of that boy's ability to connect with her and to recognize, without language, the cruelty

---

the altar for prayer, or to join the church. This is an opportunity for specific prayer, particularly on matters that are not public.

of her situation at that time. But, just as *knowing* can alert a child to harm, it can also guide them to safety.

"My *knowing* is how to spot joy," Bertice shared.

A point of personal privilege is that I love that I've come to be surrounded by so many joyful women. I wrote in my 2022 book, *Cultivating Joyful Learning Spaces for Black Girls: Insights into Interrupting School Pushout*, that while joy is often elusive for many girls in schools, as was the case for me, it is an important part of fostering belonging for our youth. In the book, I present a framework that educators can use to create a learning environment that facilitates belonging for Black girls and other students. The framework features an intentional emphasis on taking actions that counter school pushout through a critical element of childhood development: cultivating the "righteous mind" by designing learning spaces that allow girls to bring their full selves to school and to ask questions that increase their connection to the material. This is done through a rigorous curriculum, diverse faculty representation, and a clean and welcoming physical learning environment. The righteous mind is unobstructed, and therefore able to exercise the full realm of possibility. It can grow and expand with the information that it's fed, to create spaces for healing, for learning, and for joy.

I asked Bertice: "When you said your sense of knowing has allowed you to identify other people who *know* . . . are you leveraging their joy as a potential way to connect with them?"

"Yeah," she confirmed. "Because that vibrates higher than anger, hatred, jealousy, resentment . . . joy vibrates so much higher. If you can turn that joy into the pathway for everybody, then everybody succeeds. When people would say, 'What do you want to be when you grow up?' I remember telling them, *'Happy'* . . . because it looked like a job that nobody I know had."

Listening to her made me think about *knowing* as a superpower for girls. By my definition, a superpower is the ability to hone a skill that goes beyond the usual human capacity. They extend the boundaries of what is known and elevate their beholder to a unique status. That status, as a function of these special abilities, provides power—not to dominate over others, but to build and transform relationships, institutions, and conditions. The ability to activate presentational and experiential knowing through storytelling, imagery, mindfulness, and recall are examples of how simple ideas born in the hearts of girls can flourish to transform whole societies. Anna Elizabeth Dickinson, born in 1842, began advocating for human rights and the abolition of slavery when she was just twelve years old. As a White girl, she was rightly horrified by an article about a Kentucky teacher who was tarred and feathered for opposing slavery. Undeterred, she continued to fight against the immorality of slavery and its horrors. By the time she was seventeen, Dickinson was not only writing letters to newspapers opposing slavery, she was openly speaking out against racism and sexism with such force that she was invited to address Congress and President Abraham Lincoln.[29]

Girls' *knowing* is what gives them the audacity to see and experience one condition and imagine another. It gives them the vision and courage to challenge conventional notions of what is possible for them as girls. It is what allowed professional tennis player Billie Jean King, who at the age of eleven switched from softball to tennis because her family considered it a more "ladylike" sport, to transform the sport and ultimately realize her vision of becoming the "best tennis player in the world."[30] Despite an onslaught of gender bias and naysayers, King went on to be the world's top-ranked women's tennis player for six of the ten years between 1966 and 1975—even beating John Riggs, a vocal misogynist and self-described "male chauvinist," in a Battle of the Sexes tennis match in 1973.[31] She knew women could be recognized as world-class athletes, then she proved it to be true. But this *knowing* does not play out only in sports. It's girls' *knowing* that is activated when they join forces to lead a march at their school, pray for or speak up on behalf of another person they see being harmed, say hello to a lonely person, or draw a picture for someone experiencing sadness. This *knowing* reflects an offering much stronger than the forces that might seek to dim a girl's light. Women who become powerful agents for equity, justice, and human dignity begin that journey as girls.

"We always have a sense of *knowing,*" Bertice said to me. "But we get stuck on trying to attribute wisdom like that to an older person."

"I actually think of wisdom as something available to anyone at any age," I said.

Age may often be used as an indicator of wisdom, due to a commonly held association between chronology, experience, and perspective gain from lessons learned. But anyone who has ever met an old fool knows that age and wisdom are not intrinsically linked. Wisdom is when knowledge and experience inform judgment that is sound and that leads to a beneficial outcome. Girls execute wisdom each day in ways that benefit society, even when it requires them to sacrifice a piece of their innocence. For example, on May 25, 2020, a forty-six-year-old Black man was killed by the police in Minneapolis, MN. Choked to death by a police officer in a grand and heinous display of excessive force, George Floyd—whose last words were, "I can't breathe" —became the center of a global rallying cry against the egregious ways that Black people in the United States experience state violence. And the only reason it went viral for the world to see is because seventeen-year-old Darnella Frazier recorded it all.

Darnella posted the video on her social media accounts along with the caption: "They killed him right in front of cup foods over south on 38th and Chicago!! No type of sympathy </3 </3 #POLICEBRUTALITY."[32]

Though she was later awarded a Pulitzer Prize for her brave act of recording and using her platforms to call attention, to such brutality, her Black girl magic came with a price.[33] In an interview, describing the incident, she said, through tears, "It is so traumatizing."[34] In a statement released by her attorney, Darnella shared, "I opened my phone and I started recording because I knew if I didn't, no one would believe me."[35] She had the wisdom to know that documentation—and formally bearing witness to harm—was power, especially in a world that would surely try to gaslight her into believing that she had not just witnessed murder. Leading with this knowing, she shared her evidence with the world—which was brave. But I want adults who work with girls to activate that *knowing* within our girls *without the trauma.* I want a world, for example, in which Darnella would not have had to witness murder to know that the world cares about Black people's lives. I want a world in which Malala Yousafzai, Pakistani advocate for educational equity, would not have had to, at the age of twelve, been shot at by a Taliban member for people to understand the importance of defending girls' access to education globally.[36]

Everyone has an ACE Score, some exposure to trauma as a child, but I want us to instill in girls the value of *knowing* as a tool for healing.[37] This is especially important when addressing transgenerational trauma, which is the collective, unresolved, and disenfranchised grief passed on from generation to generation. Also known as *historical trauma,* transgenerational trauma can be rooted in massive, historical acts of violence such as the transatlantic slave trade, the Jewish Holocaust, or violence associated with colonization and imperialism. How these experiences are passed on from one generation to the next—through narrative storytelling, historical artifacts and other documentation, foods, migration patterns, and so on—informs how we shape communities and understand our roles as adults who work with children and adolescents. It connects us in spirit, which is the cornerstone of *knowing.*

"It's a mysticism we're after!" Bertice exclaimed. "The sacred."

"*That* I understand," I said.

In 2015, I had written a paper on the importance of sacred inquiry when working with Black girls in juvenile detention halls. It was the foundation for my clarion call to engage Black girls as "sacred and loved."

"In order for us to transform the conditions of girls, especially those in crisis, we have to engage in *sacred* inquiry to tap into the unseen, unrecognized genius of our girls," I said.

To see girls—and other children—as sacred, we must abandon the stereotypes and tropes that govern what we think about them. A sacred inquiry is one that recognizes a Divine presence in the body and environment in which we situate girls. A sacred inquiry means that we protect the environment such that it elevates love, rather than fear. It is designed to guide us toward understanding that all children are our beloveds, and that not one of them is disposable. When we act as if our girls are sacred, we build institutions that are rooted in love.

"That's the *knowing!*" Bertice exclaimed with glee.

To engage in sacred inquiry, we must encourage our girls to tap into their extended ways of knowing. Parents and educators must start early and invite them to embrace their questions, to ask them, and then to find answers to them. Adults can start this process by asking questions ourselves. We must encourage girls to form questions about current events in their own lives and in the public domain. For example, ask them: What do you see? What does that mean to you? How do you feel about that? Why are your feelings about that important? What do you want to know about this? This is something that can begin when girls are very young. The socialization that occurs among girls, such as speaking timidly, can sometimes prevent them from feeling that their questions are acceptable or valid. And in some instances, when girls *do* ask questions with force, they are met with punishment and or swift reprimand. *Pushout* features stories of girls in detention facilities who were reprimanded for asking questions, even in their juvenile court classrooms. If their questions were perceived as an affront to the authority of the teacher, they could face severe consequences, even if the questions were for clarification. So instead of asking girls (who are just as curious as everyone else) to hold their questions, think about their questions as an invitation for adults to rigorously engage them. This is how parents, educators, and society at large can foster critical thinking among girls. This is how those of us who work with girls can help them begin to locate themselves in the broader conversations that impact their lives.

We invest in girls by teaching them that their voices are valuable. We should release them from the shackles of believing that their voices are valid only if they're responding to the conditions of other people. It took generations to condition girls to believe that they needed to lead discourses on justice by centering on the well-being of boys, and we are only recently using intentional programming, leadership development, and narrative-shifting work to show girls that there is another way. Adults who work with girls need to let them know that their ability to express their own well-being as it relates to their bodies, spirits, and minds is as critical as speaking up to protect others in their communities and families. Do this by demonstrating to them that articulating their thoughts, feelings, and ideas is an essential function for girls and women in our society. Ask them often how they know things. Is it from reading? Is it because they heard of it from someone? Is it from something they've seen? A story they were told? An image that they saw? Teach them the robust learning that comes from familiarizing themselves with the way people come to know information. We should also teach girls to empower their voices, and not weaponize them. Girls' voices can be used to do more than just articulate pain. They can be a source of power. Weaponizing one's voice means to use it to harm someone else. Tapping into the multidimensional power of one's voice allows for girls to understand their capacity for communication as sacred and to use this tool as a source for uplifting rather than undermining others around them, or themselves.

Adults who work with girls, or who are raising them, must unapologetically use our resources to support programs (through funding, volunteer work, spreading the word about their existence, and other means) designed to grow girls' capacities to embrace all of the different ways that *knowing* is possible. For example, A Long Walk Home, a nonprofit organization based in Chicago dedicated to empowering youth to end violence against women and girls, uses photography and play to facilitate *knowing* among survivors of sexual violence.[38] Latinas y Lideres, an organization based in the Dominican Republic dedicated to empowering and inspiring girls from local underresourced communities, activates girls' *knowing* through music and softball.[39] Justice for Black Girls, a virtually based nonprofit organization dedicated to disrupting systems that harm Black girls in the U.S., anchors its facilitation of girls' *knowing* in creative expression (for example, role play), education, and advocacy on social media.[40] The more we develop partnerships with, invest in, and amplify the importance of these organizations, the faster society will embrace a popular culture of celebrating the depth and breadth of knowledge that our girls hold.

In 2019, I visited Atlanta with Mahogany. She was just beginning her sophomore year of high school, and I was amid a tour of Historically Black Colleges and Universities to discuss the *Pushout* documentary film. For this stretch of the tour, I was at the Atlanta University Center to screen the film at Clark Atlanta University and deliver a lecture for the Social Justice Program at Spelman College on my book *Sing a Rhythm, Dance a Blues*. I brought Mahogany with me this time because I knew that she would soon be exploring colleges for her own study, and I wanted to give her an early look at schools in Atlanta. Just before my lecture, we were walking along the oval on Spelman's campus, the central part of campus where administrative buildings, dormitories, and classrooms meet, when Mahogany stopped in her tracks. She stood there, with her eyes closed, and took a couple of breaths.

"What?" I asked. "You like it here?"

She opened her eyes and said, "I want to go here."

"Okay," I said. "You can apply, but we'll see. You'll have a lot of choices, I'm sure, so we'll see where you land."

Students often declare a "first choice" for college before they've seen the breadth of options available to them. While I acknowledged that she liked the school, I also flagged that things might change.

"You're still early in your process," I said. "You might change your mind."

"I'm going to go here," she said with certainty.

Mahogany graduated from Spelman College as part of the Class of 2025.

When girls know, they *know*. It's our job as adults to move out of their way.

2

ELEVATE PURPOSE OVER PUNISHMENT

Find out who you are and do it on purpose.

—Dolly Parton, American country singer, songwriter, actress, and philanthropist

I have always loved libraries. Seeing them as more than just a repository for books, they have been locations for safety, for possibility, for reckoning, and for access to materials that supported my spiritual deliverance. Of course, libraries were also locations for the discovery of literature and the discussions that shape our collective worldview. For most of my adolescence, the libraries in San Francisco—and later, New York—were where I could escape, where I could find peace, where I could imagine, and where I could discover. I spent lunch breaks, free periods, and after-school hours in libraries. Enveloped in the new worlds that these books offered me, I never wanted to leave.

As a young girl, especially when I turned ten, I loved the books centered on female protagonists. Hungry for content that would feed my growing imagination with the possibility that only "sheroes" could offer, I devoured the Nancy Drew mystery series, buried myself in the Ramona the Pest series, delved into Judy Blume's collection of novels, and enjoyed many other books that made clear that girls had a voice.[1] These books were especially important because they acknowledged that girls could lead. The girls in the books I read had strong voices; they stood up for what they believed in, even if it got them in trouble. In my favorite books, girls were problem solvers. They were sisters and friends. They were annoyed and annoying. They were curious and thoughtful; artistic and messy. Together, these books offered a panoply of girlhood experiences that taught me one important thing: girls matter. But I knew from the whispers of the elders around me that my racial identity mattered as well, which made my girlhood dynamic and complex. Not being able to fully locate myself in many of these stories sent a message that the creativity and power afforded to those female protagonists were still unavailable to me. So I went searching for stories about Black girls—and I found them. I discovered *Jubilee* by Margaret Walker, *I Know Why the Caged Bird Sings* by Maya Angelou, *The Bluest Eye* by Toni Morrison, and other books that confirmed that voices like mine were also important.[2] Each of these books touched a part of me that until that time did not have voice. These books awakened my agency as a reader, as a learner, and as a Black girl. And while no story was exactly like my own, I discovered a nuance to my girlhood embedded in the stories of these fictional Black girls.

One day in the fifth grade, I was perusing books after school at a local branch of the public library. Situated near San Francisco's Saint Dominic's Church,[3] which is famous for its longevity and Gothic architecture, the library boasted large windows that protected us readers from the crisp outdoors but allowed for natural sunlight and views of carefully placed trees. As with most libraries, the scent of books—old and new—filled the air, complemented by a smattering of whispers. At that time, the racks in the center of the room rotated, so I loved to twirl them until a book looked interesting enough for me to stop and read the back cover or inside flap. That afternoon, it seemed that one of the Young

Adult racks—my favorite—contained only books that I'd already read, so I was compelled to try a different one. Almost immediately, I spotted a tattered copy of Ntozake Shange's *For Colored Girls Who Considered Suicide / When the Rainbow Is Enuf*. The cover had an illustration of Shange—a brown-skinned young woman with her head turned to the side and hair covered in a scarf, looking off into the distance. She looked familiar to me, like aunties and the older girls I'd seen at the park—like all of us and none of us at the same time.

It was the title of the book that grabbed my attention first. I wondered why someone would use the term "colored." As a child of the Bay Area in the 1970s, I only knew of "Black" people. To me, the term "colored" felt like it belonged to another era, not to the post–Black Panther Party Fillmore District, which was home to the library where I found this book. As one of the primary locations where Black people lived in the city after World War II, the Fillmore District was home to family life and significant social movements in the twentieth century. The Black Panther Party, founded in Oakland, California, in 1966, coupled with the cultural nationalism of that time, which led Black people to wear Afros with pride—in the rain, fog, or sunshine—and to critique structures of oppression, sent waves of consciousness through the Bay Area. In 1968, the same year that the Summer Olympics in Mexico City featured Black American gold and bronze medalists Tommie Smith and John Carlos thrusting Black Power fists into the air in protest against the ongoing racism experienced by most African Americans, the nation's first Black Studies Department was established at San Francisco State University. It was not uncommon to see Black people moving, living, claiming, and redefining their identities in a specific, cherished, and natural way. To be "colored" felt like the antiquated language of the Jim Crow era. "Blackness" is what I understood in my early adolescence.

Do people still refer to Black people as colored? I wondered. *And why are they thinking about suicide?*

Unfortunately, even at that young age, the concept of suicide was not foreign to me. Though acts of violence from predators that threatened to take life were more prevalent, when I was eight or nine years old, I'd heard about a boy from our neighborhood who was found hanging in a yard. Some of the elders cut their eyes when recounting the incident. My babysitter at the time hailed from Shreveport, Louisiana. Her Southern drawl and acute radar for anti-Blackness held an especially doubtful tone with respect to the "accidental" nature of his death. Her intuition likely led her to suspect something more sinister, but since news from Black communities didn't always make the *San Francisco Chronicle,* which was the most widely circulated newspaper, all I knew was to trust what I had been told.

Was suicide really taking one's own life? Or were there other things that happened to drive people into a depression so deep that death is seen as the only pathway out of despair? I didn't have an answer, but the concept of Black girls dying this way scared me—even as it was familiar, since my religion class at the time taught it as a sin. So while I stared at the cover of *For Colored Girls* in the library every time I went in after that first encounter with the book, it would be years before I would open it and read it.

I hesitated to read that book because I felt it might contain truths that would disrupt what I had learned to trust for my survival. I avoided it for the same reason that so many people today choose to ignore the plight of our girls—we convince ourselves that they don't need us. Girls have been positioned to be seen and not heard—and because their needs are not often the focus in public policy or discourse, adults assume girls are doing fine if they just stay quiet or continue to perform well in school. The 1970s and 1980s—the decades during which I spent my childhood and most of my adolescence—predated public conversations about childhood trauma, or the mental health and wellness of children. So I was convinced by the age of eleven that the mental stress of witnessing intimate partner violence, of living as a survivor of sexual violence, of being parentified as the eldest girl child of five children born to a single mother, and other challenges I navigated were moot.[4] I had to trust the confident whispers of children and the small tidbits I could pry from adults about "girlhood," especially as it was being experienced in my body. I had to trust that despite my challenges, I would be fine. I did my chores. I was an A student. I could draw. I could read. I could dance and play sports. I was "fine." Right?

At a very early age, people had come into my life and violated my body and my trust. Harm doers had told me that I had no power. They labeled me as "illegitimate" as soon as I was born because my mother was single and my father was not an active parent. By age six, I had learned that my young body was not seen as worthy of protection and that it could be used as a playground for the sexual exploration of older boys and men—even those who were related to me. Predators who were fighting their own demons decided to throw some my way and threatened to kill me or my mother if I ever said anything about the abuse. So I was quiet, even when my mind was racing. But in the library, I could choose a different path. I could place myself in narratives that positioned my life as not only legitimate, but sacred and necessary. I could distract my mind and my heart from the chaos by learning new things.

I buried myself in books to escape, because in the books' worlds—in other people's narratives—I didn't have to deal with the predators in my own life. I could be a superhero. I could be a super sleuth. I could walk in the imaginary footsteps of girls who conquered their fears to challenge authority and empower their own futures. I could be bold, unemotional, and untouchable . . . I could be what society labeled as "independent." But when I engaged with those books, I had to reckon with how I had masked my pain by struggling to appear "strong" through what I was living. I never intentionally thought about pretending to be strong enough to endure the harm in my life; it was just something I did. I didn't invite the harm or the adultification that followed; but it came nonetheless.[5] This way of being in the world wasn't sustainable for me, and I knew it even at such a young age. As much as I tried, I couldn't walk safely down streets with my head buried in a book. So I stopped escaping through books and started masking by pretending the harm didn't affect me . . . and it worked, though imperfectly, for a little while.

But one afternoon, when I was in the sixth grade, a guest speaker came into my classroom to talk about childhood sexual assault. Our class was arranged with a row of desks facing the center of the room and a few rows facing the front. Each of us had a relatively unobstructed view of the chalkboard in the front of the classroom and the teacher's desk just in front of it. My seat faced the center of the classroom, so I could see not only the teacher, or in this case the presenter, but also the faces of my classmates. The presenter was announced when we returned to class after recess. Our breaths were heavy, and energy was high—and none of us had a moment to prepare for what was coming. I remember being shocked that we were going to discuss something so personal in front of everyone, and I tried to stick it out. But about halfway through the guest's presentation, something took over my body. As she spoke, I stood up, walked past the rows of students quietly listening to her presentation, and then walked out of the classroom door.

This was a new experience for me, and I was nervous. I had never walked out of a teacher's class without permission. I was typically among the most attentive students in class, especially when there was a guest speaker. But I distinctly remember feeling as if I had to run out of my skin, that I had to get out of that suffocating conversation for a breath of fresh air. I walked straight out of the classroom without looking back. I walked down the corridors and down the stairs to the school library's front entrance—my safe place. I hadn't paid attention to whether someone was following me or not, but when I turned to find no one, I was relieved. Standing at the doorway of the library, I took a couple of deep breaths. I lingered at the front door, my heart racing on pace with memories I hoped would disappear as quickly as they were formed. Anticipating that the librarian would ask why I was out of class, I never actually went inside. Instead, I turned back and slowly headed in the direction of my classroom, where the guest presenter and my classmates were still talking. I stood outside of the door and stared at a table displaying student artwork, including many pieces of my own.

After a while, another student came out to ask me to come back inside. Begrudgingly, yet obediently, I followed the other student back inside of the classroom and returned to my seat. I tried to avoid eye contact with the other students, but I could feel their eyes—and the eyes of my teacher—watching me.

"Are you okay?" a few students whispered.

I nodded "yes" to each of them, but then quickly returned my eyes to the top of the wooden desk in front of me.

"Leave her alone . . . she just wanted to leave because she's probably been through it," said Anna, a classmate who sat across from me.

"I just wanted to leave," I clarified.

"You just wanted to leave because it probably happened to *you,*" Anna pressed on defiantly. I was affixing a mask that she was determined to unhinge.

Anna was a full-figured girl with a very developed body at eleven years old. Like most of the girls in my class, we had experienced early-onset puberty and had curves that the little White girls in the books I read were praying to God for. We didn't have to pray to "increase our busts." The breasts were abundant.

"No," I lied. "I just needed fresh air."

"Because it happened to you," she insisted.

I was so angry with her at that moment. In hindsight, she may have been trying to protect me from the probes of other students, but I was still furious with her. How dare she put me out there like that? I never admitted that she was right, instead rolling my eyes at her as a signal for her to mind her own business. Ultimately, she did stop challenging me publicly—probably satisfied that she got the last word. Thinking back on it, she likely recognized the thing that I had yet to realize—that I was not alone. But I protected myself by pretending that I was okay and focusing on my schoolwork. I didn't know how to heal, and I wasn't sure anyone cared. In my young mind, I was all alone on that journey, and even if I didn't know how, I thought healing would somehow "just happen."

Then one day, the fortress that I'd built to protect myself started to crack. After recess, my entire class was told to be on our best behavior for a special presentation. Another guest speaker was coming to our class. Great! Not long after, a woman walked to the front of the classroom and introduced herself as Lois Loofbourrow.

The classroom seating chart had been rearranged, and I was now seated in the front row, my hands placed neatly on my desk. Looking up at her from behind my glasses, I noticed her blond bob haircut and piercing blue eyes as she paced back and forth in front of me. She smiled brightly, spoke firmly, and stared at me a few times. She was there to tell my classmates and me about a highly competitive summer program at an affluent private school in the wealthy neighborhood of Pacific Heights—a place where few people I knew dared to venture, where mansions sprawled along streets and down meticulously kept hillsides. The program, called Summerbridge, invited high-performing students entering the seventh and eighth grades from schools across the city to attend a six-week intensive summer school program.[6] This wasn't an ordinary summer school program, though.

"You'll be taught by high school and college students," she said.

That's cool, I thought.

"You will see that it's cool to be smart," she said.

Well, that's better than being teased for getting good grades, I thought.

She continued, "You will take academic classes in the morning and then you get electives in the afternoon that are fun . . . blah, blah . . . and you can play games like warball, blah, blah . . ."

What's warball? I thought.

"And you can go to Yosemite National Park for a week . . ."

I perked up. We'd get to go to a national park for a whole week? I'd never been on a vacation, let alone for an entire week before. I didn't know where Yosemite was, but I knew that it was a break from the monotony of my routine at the time, which consisted of school, homework, babysitting younger siblings, doing twelve loads of laundry each week, and cleaning that old lady's home.

Sign me up! I thought.

I applied to the program and, after toiling over a personal essay that I hoped was good enough to get me in, I was accepted a few months later. I'd have to take classes in the summer, but I was going to Yosemite!

Of course, Yosemite was fun, but it was the least transformative part of Summerbridge San Francisco. The program changed my life in many ways. Yes, the instruction was rigorous and yes, I made lifelong friends. As a student, it was absolutely satisfying for my high performance in school to be revered as "cool." I learned a little Spanish to complement the French I'd studied as a child; and I was introduced to the strange and captivating language of Shakespeare and other literary giants whom I had never heard of before then. I fell in love with Summerbridge and became immersed in the program—as a student, admissions committee member, tutor, teacher, and later as part of the teaching team to install the program in New Orleans. At Summerbridge, I found my first crew of friends who loved the artist Prince like I did, and who loved breakdancing and the melodrama of 1980s R&B. I discovered my voice as a young educator and the value of educational advocacy. But the most valuable lessons I took away from my involvement with the program were centered around the lives of girls, including myself.

As a fifteen-year-old first-year high school teacher in the program, I met Maria—one of the collegiate-level teachers. One day she made an announcement.

"Today after school, I'm hosting a special meeting in the library," she said to the group of rising seventh through ninth graders assembled before her. "It's just for girls to talk about their experiences."

Maria was a petite young woman whose family had recently come to the United States from Central America. She and I had shared some fun moments, and I found myself gravitating toward her wide smile and sharp analysis. She was smart and clever—just like the girls in the books I'd read as a younger girl. She was a first-generation college student, as I aspired to be at the time, so I figured that she'd understood some of the hurdles I'd have to face to get there. Maria was always patient with my questions about college, taking her time to answer my questions not only about process but also about the environment. I really liked her. I trusted her. So when she stood up during the all-school meeting and invited only girls to assemble in the library later that afternoon if they wanted to "talk about the experiences of other girls," I thought that I should probably go.

That afternoon, I walked into the library and saw Maria sitting with a small group of about six other girls from the program. The center of the library had a small amphitheater-style staircase that created space for a stage, if needed. But the girls were seated at its base, some sitting "crisscross applesauce," others with their legs outstretched. No one was elevated above anyone else and everyone was quiet. Maria and I exchanged smiles when I walked in, but I motioned that I would just need a few minutes before joining. She nodded.

I walked past the group and toward a collection of books to the side of the amphitheater stairs, still within earshot of the conversation Maria would be leading. I don't know why I didn't just go in and sit down. Instead, I acted out a whole scenario of *pretending* to need a book (likely for a lesson plan) before I could do anything else. I made sure to avoid eye contact with Maria and each of the other girls as I searched for this elusive "book."

Finally, Maria secured the doors to the library by posting a "Meeting in Progress" note, then opened the conversation by establishing it as a safe space for girls to share their experiences. She invited girls to think about what it was like to exist in a "girl body," and how it might shape who they were. I could feel my heart racing as she spoke, especially when she shared her own story of surviving sexual violence.

"One in five girls report experiencing rape and sexual assault," she said. "So I know, just by the number of girls in this room, that I'm not alone."

I felt naked.

The little girl that I had protected from considering suicide—when the rainbow is enuf—began to claw her way out. I tried to suppress her, but she was exposed.

How does she know? I thought. *How could she be so certain? One in five?*

My mind was racing almost as fast as my heart. I was wrecked and conflicted. On the one hand, I was devastated that so many others knew my pain. One in five. That's a lot of girls and that's not even everyone. That number only included reported cases. But on the other hand, I was relieved that I wasn't some freak, some anomalous creature. Immediately, that conversation allowed me to understand my situation differently. The provocation was not me or my body, but rather the adults who caused harm and the society that normalized such a heinous experience for me and other children. I was also relieved that *not* being the only one meant that, according to Maria, I could heal. At that point, I stopped pretending to be an unassuming bystander and joined the group.

Embedded in each of the girls' personal stories of exploitation and violence was a story of masking and resilience. I had been masking by pretending that the pain didn't affect me. My mask was made of armor. I was pretending to be emotionally stronger than I was. Others were masking in similar ways, or by using drugs, sex, or other activities to quash pain and appear to be at peace. After the meeting with Maria, the mask that I set in place in the sixth grade began to detach.

Approximately one-third of female survivors of rape report having experienced it for the first time when they were between the ages of eleven and seventeen.[7] Most of these incidents go unreported—as mine did—so the estimated number of survivors masking (as I was) is much greater. Knowing this information did not make my life easier, nor did it immediately prevent future acts of sexual assault from occurring. But it provided me with a lens through which to view and understand why investing in girls is not only important, but critical to the well-being of our core institutions—including the first one, which is the family. This information has empowered me to connect with girls around the world—from girls in the Bay Area of California who have survived commercial sex trafficking to the girls in Kilgoris, Kenya, who described education as a disruptor of childhood marriage and female genital mutilation.

One afternoon in the early 2010s, in a dark and quiet classroom in the Central Valley of California, I was speaking with a small group of high-school-age girls, about four of them, most of whom were from migrant families that had come to California in search of a better life. I enjoyed locating focus groups at schools, since that is the territory girls are most familiar with, so we assembled in a school classroom on a Saturday morning. We sat in a large circle, with a few desks between us as they faced each other. The girls, first-generation English speakers, sat quietly with me as I led a small focus group on the health concerns of girls whose families had been impacted by incarceration and detention. I was working on research as a consultant for a larger project that examined the health impacts of carceral systems. I opened the conversation by inviting the girls to share any initial thoughts or questions they had. At first, the girls just stared at me. I began to grow anxious that connecting with them would be more difficult than usual. It typically takes a few minutes for girls to warm up during a focus group, but I worried that language barriers might also be a factor. I smiled at the girls and reviewed the protocols of the focus group—I explained the study, reviewed the consent forms, offered them snacks, and invited everyone to get comfortable. Slowly, I watched the icy exteriors melt on each of the girls. I asked them to introduce themselves before their offerings.

Finally, a girl raised her hand, and introduced herself. She was small in stature, with long dark hair framing her face and cascading over her shoulders. Her large eyes were lined in heavy black eyeliner and mascara, making her stare even more piercing as she shared what she was looking forward to discussing with me that day.

"I want to talk about how we can get people to listen," she said. "No one believes us when we tell them what we've been through."

I nodded. She didn't have to explain more . . . I already knew the painful feeling of people not believing you or threatening your life—and those you love—if you dare to say anything about the harm you are experiencing.

The thing that I learned in the library with Maria is the thing that allows me to know, with certainty, that girls are uniquely positioned to see the possibilities of a truly just society. This is because they experience life at the intersection of multiple identities that render them vulnerable to harm in a world that has been structured to elevate—primarily—the interests of men and boys. The "unique" positionality of girls is simply one of the outcomes of *knowing* from the margins. Girls are able to see possibility along the landscape of opportunity because they are pushed off of so many roads leading to it. When girls do not experience equal access to something, they are able to identify that issue as a gap. Our job, as adults who work with them, is to help fill those gaps.

West African scholar and healer Malidoma Somé wrote, in a description of the celebration that accompanies a pregnancy in his village in Burkina Faso: "Everyone asks, 'Why is this person being sent to us at this time? What gifts will this person have that our community needs?'"[8] An individual's purpose is a question pondered by everyone in the village because they all play a role in supporting it. "The *community* exists, in part, to safeguard the purpose of each person within it and to awaken the memory of that purpose by recognizing the unique gifts each individual brings to this world," Somé writes.[9] I believe that purpose we feel, and which we ultimately manifest in our human form, is assigned by the Creator, which is why I refer to my purpose as my "Divine Assignment." It's not something I can deny—it's the reason I believe I was put on Earth at this time. My early experiences with various forms of violence, neglect, and economic and social inequality catalyzed my interest in social justice, which led me to an awareness of my Divine Assignment, my *raison d'être,* early on in life. Even when the specifics were murky, I always knew that I'd do *something*—to create a more just world for children, and specifically girls. I never saw my work as combative or in conflict with the work to advance the well-being of boys or children across the gender spectrum. In fact, my approach to producing research and other scholarship, teaching, advocacy, and philanthropy has always been additive and specific, because ensuring the wellness of our girls is the only way to ensure we are reaching *all* children in an inherently and defiantly patriarchal social structure. Because ours is a patriarchal society, the measures of success will almost always default to those that involve and impact men and boys. Framing gauges of our success that center on girls and gender-expansive or nonbinary youth ensures that when the goal is to reach *all* youth, there are specific and appropriate accountability measures in place.

Over the years, I have received letters and emails from people incredulously demanding to know: how dare I demand an investment in girls when there were "more pressing" matters of concern? They would go on to compare my work and articulations of the plight of girls to the plight of boys, and deny that we have the capacity to address two things at once. Upon publishing a short essay in *Essence* magazine on the experiences of incarcerated girls in the late 1990s, I received a handwritten letter in the mail from a man who asked, *Where do you get the nerve talking about girls when there are so many Black men locked up?* I looked at the letter, heartbroken that someone would interpret my effort to shine a light on the experiences of girls as a denial of the pain experienced by men (and boys) from the same communities as the girls I was focused on. Over time, I was met with this question in various forms—by audience members at lectures and presentations, by reporters. They wanted to know why I focused on girls in my work, and who did I think I was?

My response has always been the same, because I know my purpose. Who am I *not* to demand a deeper investment in our girls? I know that girls experience a unique, gender-based form of violence that often floats below the radar of public imagination and concern as it is reflected in policy, law, practice, and entertainment. Many times, it's sexual, but often it's not. It's personal, and it's cultural. It's economic. It's political. It's educational. It's institutional.

The 2019 documentary film *Pushout: The Criminalization of Black Girls in Schools* was based on *Pushout* and *Sing a Rhythm, Dance a Blues,* two of my books that explore how Black girls experience policies, practices, conditions, and a prevailing consciousness that renders them vulnerable to future contact with the criminal legal system.[10] In that film, I mentioned that I had a "high ACE score"—a measure of childhood trauma—in a classroom filled with about twenty teenage girls who were surviving some of life's biggest challenges—from poverty and hunger to sexual and physical violence—all before the age of eighteen. These girls graciously participated in the film to show, with their own stories, that marginalization from school is a function of far greater forces than simply a "bad attitude," which is what Black girls are often accused of having in school and other settings—and they are punished for it. The film examines how girls interpret and navigate the circumstances of their lives when the odds are stacked against them.

Perhaps viewers of the film can sense my hesitation in revealing my actual ACE number on-screen at the time. Personally, my discomfort is palpable every time I watch myself in the film. I was nearly shaking while revealing that I had a high score, and I didn't have it in me to share what my specific traumas were. I have since come to realize that my ACE score is the reason my empathy for our nation's girls is unflappable. My score is one of the reasons that I am uniquely qualified to lead organizations and advocacy efforts that ensure our girls are not marginalized in conversations about social policy. My score is one of the reasons that I *care* so much. It's the reason I clearly see my purpose. Someone with a score of 4 out of 10 is more likely to attempt suicide, more likely to develop a dependence and/or addiction to alcohol and other drugs, and more likely to have their life span shortened by approximately twenty years.[11] My high ACE score is sometimes detectable in my speech. My therapist noted that she can tell when

I'm triggered, even in the delivery of my TED Talk on why Black girls are targeted for punishment in school, because my breathing shifts when I'm discussing my experience with neglect and abuse.[12] It is something that I will seek to recover from for the rest of my life—but I am committed to that healing, and to the prevention of harm to other girls and young people. My ACE score is 7. Some of the girls gathered in the room for the *Pushout* documentary had a score of 10.

During the film's production, it wasn't as important for me to share what my number was as it was to share that having a high ACE score (4 or higher) does not automatically translate to a life of pain and sorrow. It is important both to contextualize the trauma in the context of other structural barriers to well-being, and to understand that, with the intervention of protective factors, such as therapy and sports, and people, such as counselors, mentors, and coaches, recovery is absolutely possible.

My understanding of the stress of being an eldest girl child with tremendous domestic responsibility, experiencing sexual violence, being subjected to racialized gender bias that reduced my expressions of femininity to stereotypes and tropes rooted in hypersexualization, and being subjected to the "strong Black woman" trope have allowed me to walk into rooms of young people in communities across the world—from Indigenous reservations on the West Coast to brownstones on the East Coast and shotgun houses in the South; from the slums of Nigeria to colleges in India and Costa Rica—and to be in conversation with young people and empathize with their plights. Wherever I have been in the world, girls have conveyed the same message: they want adults to invest in their well-being by teaching them truthfully, by steering them toward paths to help them care for themselves and their future families, by listening to them, and by giving them the tools they need to be effective leaders, if they so choose. The girls I have met want adults to love them and show it through their actions.

They don't want adults to treat them as disposable because they've been hurt. They want empathy.

Empathy makes the connection to a young person real, because it amplifies *why* adults take the actions they do and move resources the way that they do. It moves us away from interpreting disparity as a function of the natural order of things, and instead, invites us to explore *why* these conditions exist. It's *empathy* that has allowed me to understand the unique vulnerabilities of girls in schools across the nation. Empathy also created space for me to commit to their well-being, and to amplify the amazing transformations in performance and life outcomes that happen in their lives when we do. Talking to girls about their experiences, for instance, created space to address the policing of girls' bodies through dress codes and to engage in the development of remedies to gender-based violence in schools. Once advocates and researchers demanded that educational institutions move past responding to student behavior with only punitive and exclusionary practices, there was room for empathetic responses to negative student behavior, problematic conditions like "Slap Ass Fridays"—where girls would have to endure the unwanted and unprovoked act of having their bottoms smacked by boys—were met with accountability, not disbelief or accusations of "false reporting."[13] Following a report by the Alliance for Girls in Oakland, California, in which middle school girls described being routinely subjected to this form of sexual harassment, the school board developed a policy, rooted in restorative approaches, that included revamping the procedures for reporting sexual harassment, interrogation of truancy claims in cases involving girls who were seeking to avoid harassment in schools, and opportunities to educate all students about consent and the violative nature of unwanted flirtation. Empathy invites us to see not just the harm, but also the remedies. It reveals that these conditions are too much for any child, and we're doing too little to stop it.

* * *

Girls—their bodies and their aptitude for decision-making—are vulnerable to regressive policies before they can even form an articulation of their human experiences on their own. The U.S. Constitution does not explicitly protect women's rights—and that extends to girls. Child marriage remains legal in thirty-six states and U.S. territories, with most of the United States allowing marriage before the age of eighteen.[14] The absence of an explicit legal foundation makes it hard to protect girls from this practice. In 2018, Delaware and New Jersey became the first two states to end child marriage, followed by American Samoa later that same year. Between 2020 and 2024, the U.S. Virgin Islands, Pennsylvania, Minnesota, Rhode Island, New York, Massachusetts, Vermont, Connecticut, Michigan, Washington, Virginia, and New Hampshire all ended child marriage.[15] Between 2010 and 2018, more than 300,000 children, some as young as ten years old, were married in the U.S., with the majority of these cases being girls who were married to adult men.[16] And that's just one example. *When and how* we see girls informs their life trajectories. Greta Thunberg's early activism at fifteen years old to address the carbon footprint of her family and community paved the way for her to become a global environmental and climate change activist. At just eleven years old, Marley Dias demanded that her school include more books with Black girls as main characters, charting a path for her to launch a national #1000BlackGirlBooks campaign and become a leading global voice on the importance of diversity in children's literature. As case after case of girls who have "changed the world" would suggest, girls who are seen and supported with a platform to exercise their leadership go on toward the realization of their purpose in life.

Teens who have a strong sense of purpose are more likely to

have a positive outlook on life.[17] My experiences working with girls over the years have revealed that girls who know their purpose are a lot harder to gaslight—at home, at work, at play, or at rest. They are harder to manipulate. According to the *Harvard Business Review,* people with a strong sense of purpose at younger ages tend to be more resilient against setbacks, which is an essential element of seeking healing from the dangers and/or harms that people inevitably confront in life.[18] Investing in girls such that they have the tools to lean into their purpose, which includes a sense of knowing, education, mentorship, advocates, community, etc., allows them to fully explore not only their own processes for self-regulation, but also their ability to demand that the adults and decision-makers in their communities help them when they need it.[19] Some, such as parents and other adults who want to protect the innocence of children, may argue that it shouldn't be the responsibility of girls to ask people to help them—that adults should simply see when girls need help and respond accordingly. Of course, adults *should* help girls! But if adults falter, we need to equip girls with the tools to demand what they need to see their own worth, exercise their agency, and work to identify safe adults (adults who do not harm children) who can guide them toward the execution of their purpose.

This is not about equipping girls solely for their labor or other contributions to society. This is about establishing the very foundations for them to experience joy and satisfaction in their lives. To be on the trajectory toward a life of satisfaction, girls need to know their purpose. As girls step fully into their purpose, they will recognize the unique value of their voices and their perspectives, which help them to align their actions accordingly. I've met many girls who do *not* know their purpose—we all have! Often, they are going through the motions, not aware of their calling in life, and they flail in the face of adversity. Life's challenges are continuous, and girls may face a stream of adverse circumstances to which they can more adeptly respond when they are clear about why they are alive.

One's purpose can be clearest when tested. This logic also applies to girls. So it's important to encourage girls to walk in their purpose not only when they are doing well, but also when they are in trouble. This is a challenging charge because when girls encounter trouble, the adults around them tend to rely on stereotypes, tropes, or unconscious beliefs about them, which can undermine their ability to recognize promise and possibility. I witnessed this in the juvenile justice systems many times. From the mid-1990s through the 2000s, practitioners in the justice system, particularly those working in the juvenile court or probation departments, held onto what we called the "cage them, save them" mentality. This mind-set reflected the belief that in order to keep girls from returning to the dangers of the streets—the conditions that led them to the juvenile court to begin with—they needed to be locked in secure facilities.

"At least this way, girls can't get exploited," justice practitioners would often say to me.

"It's the only way we have to ensure that our girls are safe," others would say in defense of the practice of keeping girls detained in juvenile facilities for lengthy periods of time. This practice was especially prevalent in cases involving girls who were being sex trafficked.

Of course it was not the *only* way. Data show that detaining youth, even for one day, leads to conditions that threaten their safety and well-being. It was not until survivor advocates, particularly girls themselves, began to educate practitioners, researchers, and service providers around the country about their experiences that new understanding—and practices—began to take shape. When girls were encouraged by direct service providers and advocates to identify their purpose, they began to challenge the practices that deepened the harm against them. Armed with the knowledge of their experiences and an awakening to their life goals, which included interest in cosmetology, forensic science, education, and other fields, these girls became young women who would transform many approaches to girls in contact with the juvenile court system, from the Bay Area to Washington, D.C. They became heroes in their own stories.

It's always been upsetting to me that while many of the great literary classics in Western traditions, such as the *Odyssey* of Homer, celebrate a young man's hero's journey as the quintessential expression of his gifts, no such "classic" tale exists for young women. Despite this absence, my years of working with girls has shown me that a girl's purpose and her power are equally palpable when she is in her greatest trial. This does not mean that someone has to go through bad things to realize their purpose; but it does suggest the long-held human belief that in *order* to overcome life's greatest challenges, a person needs to tap into their core values and beliefs. This journey is never completed alone. Even as it is a deeply personal journey—physically, emotionally, spiritually, and intellectually—it is always completed with the help of others, people who serve as guides, such as mentors, and books or other resources that help to move a person toward their purpose.

People who work with girls, or who are raising or guiding them, should ask girls who they are under pressure, and what values they lean into when they are challenged. Exercising their multiple ways of knowing—including their thoughts, feelings, and intuition—helps girls access their purpose during the hardest times in their lives. Helping a girl find her purpose is one of the most important skills adults who are trusted to guide them can impart.

The key to helping girls unveil their purpose is to examine *with them* their core competencies and skills. Adults who work with girls should ask them: What feels natural? What are you good at? We often ask girls what their gift is. This question really asks about what inspires their joy and comfort. What would you do to bring yourself joy and add value to your community and/or to society? Ask girls these questions constantly and continuously, so that they are invited to dream and discover their purpose early in life. The expression of their purpose will encourage them to bring their full selves to everything they do, to be a whole person everywhere, in every scenario on their path toward a limitless future.

I was in my early thirties and leading a think tank in Berkeley, California, focused on mapping the prevalence of racial, gender, and language discrimination in employment, public contracting, and hospitals, among other segments of the public domain. As the think tank's new executive director, it was important for me to build relationships with other Black women leaders within the field, as there were not many of us. Occasionally, I would seek the mentorship of attorney Eva Paterson, one of San Francisco's leading civil rights voices. She cofounded and was then serving as the president of the Equal Justice Society, a legal advocacy organization that seeks to transform "the nation's consciousness on race through law, social science, and the arts."[20] She played an active role in mentoring me as a young Black woman and new leader in the field of civil rights research and would regularly meet with me to discuss my progress. One day over lunch, I casually mentioned my appreciation for and full-blown enchantment with the music of legendary artist and musician Prince. I had just come back from seeing Prince in concert, which I did as often as possible, and was reliving a favorite moment of the show with her. Whenever I talk about Prince, I come alive—so I was in a full state of joy as I replayed the set list, his dance moves, and something he quipped in his ad libs between songs. I made a comparison to a previous show and mentioned something about seeing him do something different at another concert. I remember the grin on her face as she listened to me go on and on.

Then she asked, "How many concerts have you been to?"

"I don't know . . . I don't count. I just go," I replied.

"You really love Prince."

I paused, chuckled, and nodded.

"You know who else loves Prince?"

I listened as she named another emerging scholar and philanthropic professional whom I wanted to meet but hadn't yet.

"You should tell him about how much you love Prince," she said.

I cringed: "I can't do that! That's my *personal* life."

"You can't live like that," she said. "Show people who you are . . . that's how you build relationships of all types."

I paused to consider what she was suggesting, and then nodded. Honestly, I thought about that conversation for months after. I had been taught by previous employers and mentors to silo my personal identity from my work—to think of work as the place where I express my intelligence, or where I demonstrate the reaches of my labor. But Prince was my joy, a special thing for *me*. At his concerts, I didn't have to know the answers to hard questions or focus on the underbelly of society. They were places where people from all walks of life came together to listen to masterful guitar playing and sultry lyrics that made us all feel desirable. Work was over *there*. Joy (and Prince) were over *here* . . . but maybe Eva had a point.

Ultimately, I decided to take a chance and at the next concert I attended, I picked up an extra program for this colleague. At our initial meeting, I greeted him with the concert program. His eyes enlarged, he let out a shriek, and then displayed a massive grin as he reached for it. He seemed surprised that I knew about his love for Prince, and I was pleased to have found another genuine fan. We carefully examined each page of the concert program and spent half of our meeting talking about Prince, but we did get to business . . . eventually. We've been friends and true colleagues ever since—holding each other accountable to our purpose over the years, and across a number of organizations.

This experience taught me that it's essential to a boundless future to bring your full self to your purpose, and that when you do, it's a critical way to secure your well-being. Being *whole* is being *well.* We don't live as compartmentalized humans, and we shouldn't be asked to do so when we enter the realm of our calling. This theme echoed for me years later, when I was doing research for my doctoral study. I came face-to-face with a sixteen-year-old survivor of sex trafficking whose eyes spoke to me with sadness, even as her mouth found a slight smile. A decade or so had passed since my interaction with Eva about bringing my full self to my work—and honestly, I was still working on it. I had done many things in the meantime, including working with Kemba Smith—a young woman who was granted presidential clemency, and eventually a full pardon, after being sentenced to 24.5 years in federal prison for crimes she did not commit—on her book *Poster Child,* about being impacted by mandatory minimum drug sentencing; writing articles for national publications and a column for *Ebony* magazine about how social policies and public perceptions impact Black girls; and leading empirical studies on economic exploitation and bias. But I hadn't yet fully connected the dots between all of the various work I produced. I still wasn't bringing my full self to the execution of my purpose.

My first book, the 2001 novel *Too Beautiful for Words,* is based on a 1998 song by The Coup, an independent hip-hop group from Oakland, called "Me and Jesus the Pimp in a '79 Granada Last Night." The song is about an Oakland-based pimp who ultimately faces the consequences of his actions. My book explores the story of a family seeking to make meaning of salvation and liberation in a city known for both its pimp culture and Black nationalist roots. I'd heard the song when it was first released and was immediately inspired to write a book from its compelling core narrative. A few weeks after my first listen, I was able to connect with "Boots" Riley, front man for The Coup and, later, the writer/director of the critically acclaimed 2018 film *Sorry to Bother You*. We agreed to meet at a diner on Lake Merritt to talk about what inspired the story. Boots arrived with sunglasses hiding his eyes, even as his freckled, butterscotch skin and large Afro, lined by his signature sideburns, clearly marked him as the person I was there to see. Dressed in jeans and a T-shirt, his casual style made it feel like I was meeting a friend.

We chatted for a while about his song. I wanted to know why he wrote it and he in turn wanted to know why I wanted to write a book about it. Our conversation covered faith, exploitation, and Black nationalism, among other political topics. I asked about his rationale for creating an antagonist in his song who wears a prosthetic arm. I'd read the antagonist's disability as a statement about his location in society. An avowed democratic socialist at the time, Boots confirmed that I was on the right track.

"You know Dr. Manning Marable?" he asked. "He wrote this book called *How Capitalism Underdeveloped Black America* . . ."

I was giddy. I studied under Manning Marable for a number of years as an undergraduate and graduate student at Columbia University, and he guided much of my early academic thinking about participatory research and what he called Contemporary Black History, the study of current phenomena and events of historical significance among and impacting Black people. He was a prolific author and beloved professor of history, though his work extended to other disciplines such as public affairs. In 1993, he had come to Columbia to revamp the African American Studies program and give it structure as the founding director of the Institute for Research in African American Studies. I, for one, was thrilled. I was a Political Science and African American Studies double major, and while I felt supported in my study of political science, my journey in African American Studies felt less secure. At the time,

I had been working as a telemarketer in Queens to support myself as a student, which meant that my commute to work from uptown Manhattan took more than an hour one way and involved transferring to three trains, followed by a ten-minute walk. I was frustrated by that experience—and not particularly talented as a telemarketer—and wanted to get back to my world of research. As soon as I learned that he was taking meetings, I scheduled one, and on a late August afternoon, I walked into his office.

I remember walking in with humility and being delighted by the kind man who greeted me from behind his desk. He wore a round, gray Afro (sometimes parted on the side like the abolitionist Frederick Douglass). His circular glasses and salt-and-pepper goatee gave him the studious look of many in the Black intelligentsia, an elite group of Black scholars who helped to shape the policies impacting the lives of Black Americans at the time. He and his friend group and cherished colleagues had written many of the books on my bookshelf. Being in his presence felt like being in the presence of a rock star. With humility, he insisted that I call him by his first name, Manning, and invited me to take a seat.

"Tell me about yourself," he said.

"I'm an African American Studies and Political Science double major," I began. I went on to tell him about my intentions for my scholarship, how I wanted to write about conditions that facilitate community development and interrogate ways for Black research to reflect a more dynamic understanding of the lived experiences of Black people.

"Music to my ears," he said. "How can I help you?"

"I need a job," I said bluntly. I wanted his tutelage, too, but as a twenty-year-old student who was three thousand miles from home, it was more essential to secure money for my basic needs.

He let out a bellowing laugh and nodded. Then he hired me on the spot, and I became part of the first cohort of students to work at the institute. From that first encounter, a mentorship and friendship developed. So when Boots shared that he had written the song with Manning's work in mind, I was eager to know more.

"There's a part of the book that talks about the symbolic value of Black businesses," Boots went on.

"I know that passage well," I said, revealing my relationship to Manning.

Boots and I discussed a primary note in Manning's book that read: *"White corporations allow Black companies to exist for symbolic value alone."*[21] Boots shared that Manning's work was the inspiration for the antagonist in his song—a man who represented a harmful figure that is allowed to exist by a structure of greater significance and power. We marveled at the serendipity of our meeting, and Boots agreed to let me develop his song into a book. What followed was the story of a seventeen-year-old girl named "Peaches" who births a son, forms an unlikely friendship with a female Black Panther, and goes on to endure a tumultuous relationship that includes sexual exploitation and violence. It was cathartic to write that book after spending years in and out of detention facilities listening to girls (and boys) share their stories of violent victimization—but I didn't know that it would also serve another purpose.

The book was often read by girls, juvenile justice reform advocates, and detained youth throughout the Bay Area and in other parts of the country. Over the next decade or so, as I became immersed in early motherhood and took on leadership of the Discrimination Research Center, the small think tank in Berkeley; became the director of research for the Thelton E. Henderson Center for Social Justice and UC Berkeley Law School; and worked for the National Office of the NAACP, all of which redirected my writing to the production of research and other reports, I let my little novel idle on the bookshelf. But God had other plans.

Back to the sixteen-year-old whom I was speaking with for my doctoral study: sitting with this young survivor, I prepared to take field notes for my study and was taken right back to that long-lost girl I called Peaches.

"Wait . . . what's your name again?" she asked before we began.

I told her my name.

"You're the one who wrote that book!" she exclaimed. She shifted in her seat and smiled. "Oh, I can talk to *you.*"

She let out a relaxed breath and began to talk freely to me about her experiences. My childhood made me familiar with the lived experiences of vulnerable girls. Those experiences led me to an interest in African American narratives, which led to my graduate studies with Manning Marable and thesis on how residential juvenile correctional facilities shaped the urban landscape for Black communities in the U.S., weakening their social infrastructure and negatively impacting community development. They also led to my work in elementary schools as a volunteer with girls, as an educator, and as a consultant with state government agencies focused on improving educational and justice outcomes for children and adolescents in California, and beyond. My research helped me understand Boots's intention with a song that I would interpret as text. This text would serve as a foundation for building a rapport with girls in carceral facilities and ultimately lead me down a road of producing books, films, and shorts on the criminalization of Black girls in schools. My worlds were fusing and roads converging in the best possible ways because *I was finally bringing my full self to my work—toward the execution of my purpose.* I was no longer compartmentalizing myself and my gifts. Instead, I was integrating them in ways that helped me heal from my traumas, and that I could channel to identify potential remedies to harmful conditions in all girls' lives. And it hasn't stopped. My research and advocacy have continued to serve as the foundation for my philanthropic support for girls.

In 2023, I published my first graphic novel, *Charisma's Turn,* a story about a girl who faces the potential of school pushout before a school counselor intervenes and helps her tap into her purpose. The story about "girls and their gifts" is intended to amplify the promise of prioritizing purpose over punishment. After years of having conversations with adults about how to end school pushout, I decided to write something for young people themselves. In return, I received notes from girls across the country—from precocious elementary students to curious high school students—praising the core thesis of the book: that girls perform better when people believe in them and direct them toward their purpose.

In 2024, the Brooklyn Children's Theater adapted the book as part of its Viola Davis Summer Program, a youth musical theater camp named for the prolific thespian, taking my graphic novel to the stage. I went to the opening night of the musical with great anticipation. I knew that the young people had worked very hard to bring Charisma's story to life. It was a beautiful production, and I had to fight back tears after watching children of all racial and ethnic groups and genders, mostly in high school, powerfully celebrate the value of a good teacher to help steward a Black girl toward her gifts. It was especially meaningful to hear the feedback from girls who played key roles in the story.

A tenth grader wrote, *"Working on* Charisma's Turn *meant that I would be able to bring and show awareness to topics like colorism and misogyny that affects Black girls everywhere on a daily basis in a way that people wouldn't feel uncomfortable or threatened by, that would hopefully make them more willing to listen and understand just some of the issues that Black girls go through."*

Another tenth grader wrote, *"First off, my experience was great. Right before the show started, I faced a major mental health setback, so coming to a place where I felt accepted and made a bunch of friends helped me so much. Playing that character meant a lot to me because she's the opposite of me, but somebody I understand. Her always putting a mask on to please others is something every Black teenage girl has to face and being able to play her really brought out that we all go through things and cope differently and it doesn't cost anything to just be nice."*

These are the testimonies that keep me on the path of my purpose. As someone who had to figure out school on her own, first as a nonnative French speaker and then as a first-generation college student, these displays of community strengthen my resolve to ensure that other girls don't have to navigate difficult spaces in the same way. I believe that everything happens in Divine Order, in alignment with God's will. I get excited when I see the young people in my life experience "full circle" moments, for instance, when aspects of their lives unexpectedly connect to make perfect sense, or when I experience these moments myself—because I know it is happening as a result of walking in alignment with our purpose.

Integration of our passions, interests, skills, and calling is a lifelong work in progress, but I have come to understand that the sooner we seek it, the greater our capacity is for actualizing it. Teaching our girls to bring their full selves to their purpose is not only okay, it's *necessary.*

"Excuse me, I just wanted to introduce myself," a young woman said to me one afternoon in the fall of 2024. I was in Chicago for a meeting and presentation when she walked up to me quietly and introduced herself. "My name is Amber."

"Nice to meet you, Amber," I said.

She was a young woman in her early twenties, with her hair pulled back neatly into a bun. A little shy in demeanor, she was rocking back and forth between her right and left foot.

"When I was fifteen, someone gave me your book," she said. "*Pushout.*"

That caught my attention, because I was immediately interested in learning about the connection between the material in *Pushout* and her work with girls in Chicago. She went on to tell me that she had read it as a teenager and was inspired to make a positive impact on the conditions of other girls in her community. She shared that she was active in programming throughout high school and was later accepted to Hampton University, where she founded an organization that she called Black Is Gold, to support Black women and girls with college and career readiness, leadership development, and mental health resources. The program has since expanded to reach girls and young women not only in Chicago, Illinois, and Hampton, Virginia, but also in Atlanta, Georgia.

I marvel that one book—or one gesture of the woman to hand her my book—could have inspired so many girls to step into their purpose, and I was particularly impressed by its impact on Amber's life. She is yet another testament to the power of providing girls with tools and then stepping out of their way. When a girl is aligned with her purpose, the impact is infinite—it reproduces and spreads beyond what we can imagine.

Investments in girls' purpose are iterative: make one and nurture its growth.

3

DISMANTLE THE STRUCTURAL BARRIERS TO HER SUCCESS

I figured out it was a social thing, what women were allowed to do. At a very young age, I decided I was not going to follow women's rules.

—Joan Jett, American singer and songwriter known as the "Godmother of Punk"

"You've been assigned to lead the new project in Louisiana," Fred said, as he grabbed a chair and dragged it into my cubicle.

Fred was a tall, light-brown man in his early sixties with a clear, deep voice. His hair was cut close to his scalp and his thin mustache was always groomed. I rarely saw him wearing anything other than a three-piece suit, tailored to fit his strong and slender stature. He was the former director of a state juvenile correctional facility and held the belief that his experience in that capacity gave him a unique insight as to why we don't want our children in these facilities. He was a no-nonsense man who had a keen palate for the delights of California's wine country, and he was working as a consultant for the National Council on Crime and Delinquency, or NCCD, the nation's oldest nonprofit criminal and juvenile justice research organization. Filled with a team of criminal justice researchers and other social scientists, the organization often led trainings for probation departments and provided technical assistance—a type of consultation to troubleshoot with agencies as they respond to specific challenges with implementation of an idea or program—to the judiciary and other stakeholders in the criminal and juvenile justice arena, via government contracts and other large-scale reform efforts.

This was my first lead on a project as part of the senior research staff at NCCD and I was proud of myself. The project, which I helped to broker, would explore ways to reduce youth recidivism in three high-crime parishes of Louisiana.

"Add me to your team," he said.

I agreed but looked at him quizzically.

As if reading my mind—or the transparency of my facial expression, he said, "I'm licensed to carry a gun."

At just twenty-five years old, I was the youngest project lead in the organization at the time. I was also the only Black woman. His reaction to my new assignment may seem extreme, but I later found out why he was so concerned. Although I had spent the summer in New Orleans as a middle school teacher for Summerbridge many years earlier, this would be the first time that I would actually have to venture out into the areas known for their more extreme racist politics. That was made clear on day one. The morning we set to launch our work in one of the neighboring parishes to New Orleans, I opened the local newspaper over breakfast and was greeted with a reality check. I was sitting with Fred and Dick, my supervisor—another older Black man who had demonstrated institutional leadership in the field of juvenile justice. They had both come down to help me launch the project. With shock and horror, I stumbled upon an ad that had been taken out to support the candidacy of David Duke, a notorious white supremacist, for a seat in Congress. Listed among a series of "accomplishments" was that he had been the grand wizard of the Ku Klux Klan. I remember looking up from the paper in disgust.

"Are they serious?" I asked, trading looks with the elder statesmen who accompanied me.

"Yes," was their collective reply. No smiles. Just clarity.

I wondered how my policy recommendations for children and adolescents caught in the web of violence and neglect could be taken seriously in a place where people openly celebrated belonging to one of the most notorious executors of vigilante violence in this nation's history. I didn't doubt myself—I knew I was qualified to lead and I knew it was important to be in the rooms where decisions were made. I just wondered what I'd have to do to get this particular community to see more than my skin color, gender, and age. I prayed for my safety, and I thanked my grandpa—as an ancestor—for sending Dick and Fred to be by my side. He knew I'd need protection, even if I didn't.

I had most recently served as an integral part of a team working on a special federal project that was exploring juvenile delinquency and the specific things that led young people into contact with the juvenile court. It was called the Comprehensive Strategy for Serious, Violent, and Chronic Juvenile Offenders—a special project of the U.S. Department of Justice's Office on Juvenile Justice and Delinquency Prevention—and was a major technical assistance project that NCCD led across the nation. That project would eventually take me to many states and communities and give me the opportunity to talk to young people in juvenile detention centers, group homes, and community-based diversion and reentry programs. For the latter part of the 1990s, I worked in Ohio, Florida, New Jersey, California, Maryland, and other areas that were grappling with how to reduce the number of young people who were chronically in contact with the juvenile court system for violent offenses. My approach was always to look at more than just whether young people were being arrested and detained. I was interested in how they were impacted by circumstances beyond their control. These included the conditions of poverty, violence, toxic climates, and poor infrastructure in their schools and neighborhoods, which sometimes led them to participate in underground economies, rendering them vulnerable to future contact with the juvenile court or criminal legal system more broadly.

It was challenging work and taught me a lot about systems, particularly about how decisions are made in large public agencies, and about how people exercise discretion at the most senior levels to reinforce their own political and social beliefs. It also taught me about the mental fortitude and focus it takes for young women to be taken seriously in largely older male dominated spaces. Not only was I a young woman, just a few years out of my master of science program, but I was a young Black woman. Many of the people I was interfacing with had no history of meaningful interactions with Black people, and I would come to learn that the only times they saw African American women my age, they were in recovery from addictions, unclothed, or being sexualized. In the recesses of their mind, that's who I was—and this mattered only because I was working in an environment that was charged with racial disparities. My analysis as a young Black woman was essential to understanding the specific structural barriers the young people impacted by the carceral and child welfare systems faced. Those barriers hindered the well-being of the young people at the center of all of our work. I was clear that these institutional leaders would hear my analysis only if they took me seriously as a scholar and technical assistance provider—if they could see me as a skilled *professional* in this area.

At this time, I was routinely in conversation with practitioners, attorneys, probation officers, prosecutors, public defenders, and the judiciary at the local and state levels. On occasion, I was also in conversation with policymakers, some of whom made it clear that they didn't understand why I needed to attend those meetings. I was there to offer my perspectives on how to improve policies for young people impacted by the juvenile court, but some public officials struggled to accept what I had to offer. Once, during a meeting with a state legislator, I sat with the NCCD team members and talked about salient issues in the juvenile court system, such as racial disparities, the absence of diversion programs, and the absence of cognitive behavioral therapy solutions for young people who had contact with the court. At the end of the meeting, as we were walking out of the door, people lined up to shake the state legislator's hand. As was customary, he walked over to the men and shook their hands one by one, thanking them for their time. When he reached the colleague beside me, he reached out his hand, shook it firmly, and glanced down at me.

"I see you brought a pretty girl with you," he said, before releasing his hand and beginning to reach out for mine.

I'm certain I frowned—I'm not known for having a poker face.

"I'm also a professional," I said.

He shook my hand—squeezing it unbearably hard, as if trying to assert his physical dominance over me—and continued with the procession. I looked at my colleague as I nursed my sore hand. He chuckled nervously and shrugged. We all needed this appointed official to do what we'd asked, and challenging him on his wretched behavior with me might jeopardize that. I felt awful and deflated. I'd worn a fitted, knee-length purple dress with a matching crocheted cardigan because it was hot outside and I wanted to remain cool. But his comments made me feel exposed. I vowed then to shift my public presentation, deciding that it was easier to change how I dressed than to try to change his treatment of women in the workplace.

After that, I shifted my entire professional wardrobe to include only items I would call "man-up gear" in an effort to make myself appear as "masculine" as possible. This amounted to no skirts, no dresses, no makeup, no heels. I already had my hair cut in a very short, natural style, so I would wear basic pantsuits, glasses, and flats to ensure that people were focused on my contributions rather than my appearance. It was the primary tool I had available to me at the time, and it would take at least a decade for me to abandon that performance as a strategy to break through the "old boys' network" that was decidedly at play. I observed many women do the same thing to downplay their femininity, wearing clothing designed to obscure their gender, or make it a nonissue. Rather than attack the culture that prevents us from being our full selves authentically, many of us resort to performance to get through the moment. I'm not disappointed in myself for having made those decisions at such a young age. I was simply working with what I had available to me at the time. However, those experiences led me to an analysis about why people with power responded to me the way they did, and what I would eventually need to do to change that. Wearing a dress or wearing pants does not change, for example, the fact that women still make only a percentage of the dollar earned by men. My decision not to wear heels did not erase the fact that there were no programs in place to divert girls who were being sex trafficked from the juvenile court system. But my presence in rooms where there were conversations and decisions being made about the development of these programs and these structures did. So I played the game—as many women before me had and many women after me would.

Don't get me wrong. I still *love* a good power pantsuit. But I want to wear one because I like it, not to avoid the vitriol or undesired comments of insecure men! It's what I want for all of us.

Aside from this introduction to the politics of presentation, the project in Louisiana was my awakening to the interplay between individual bias and the power to wield this bias. Though I had taught middle school students in Louisiana in 1991, I was now able to access elected and appointed policymakers on their playground—state government—and I found that many of them used their power to reinforce norms that sustained and/or exacerbated harm for hundreds of young people. For example, I watched as the head of a detention center forced the detainees—all of them young Black boys and girls—to stand when she walked in the room as if they were her subjects. I listened to a district attorney refer to the children who came before him as "little Black bastards," displaying his lack of empathy for the increased surveillance and lived experiences that brought them more frequently into contact with the juvenile court. I navigated a politically and racially charged environment where the criminal judge refused to meet with me as the project lead but would meet with a White woman who was my subordinate on the project. But I also watched a Black woman judge try to create conditions in her courtroom that were fair to the young people who were coming out of poverty. I partnered with a local minister and his church to help ensure that the young people in juvenile hall didn't have to share underwear, which was routinely happening at this time. I learned how public institutions such as courts, probation departments, and schools—as the primary instruments of power—could mete out or undermine justice in many ways. The complexities were enormous! I am most grateful that this project gave me an up-close look at how people with power can so vastly misinterpret the lived experiences of girls that they fail to even *offer* opportunities for them to recover from harm.

On many occasions, I would go in and talk to girls who had been arrested for prostitution or theft or other economic crimes and statutory offenses associated with their struggle to survive.[1] Most of the adults I was working with were practitioners in the juvenile court system, and only saw that young people had violated the law. They did not acknowledge, at least publicly, that young people were responding to intense levels of racialized gender violence. Instead, wardens and institutional staff placed girls in poorly lit rooms in remote parts of the facility that were surrounded by steel doors and cinder block walls. Much of the analysis about their conditions was informed by assumptions that the girls were willful participants in the crimes they were being punished for. Therefore, the court—and other practitioners along the juvenile justice continuum—often responded to delinquency by focusing solely on girls' behaviors, which were in fact responses to their conditions, their traumas, and circumstances. For example, youth gangs at the time understood that because of the War on Drugs, the risk of selling illicit substances was too great for them to take on, so, instead of selling drugs such as crack cocaine, they sold sex with the girls in their communities. The detention centers were being filled with youth in gangs, but these young people all described the same thing: a desire for family, for employment, and for education to live out their dreams.

While listening to fourteen-year-old girls describe life in sex clubs and on street corners, I wondered what would happen if decision-makers in educational, child welfare, and juvenile justice systems—and every advocate working on behalf of girls impacted by these systems—shifted focus. I wondered what would happen if we didn't focus solely on girls' *responses* to the systems and institutions causing harm in their lives, but also spent time advocating for the structures to shift so that they wouldn't cause harm in the first place. I would even find myself in tense exchanges with judges—not just in Louisiana, but in California, Ohio, New Jersey, and other communities as well—who refused to see the prostitution of girls as sexual exploitation, or drug crimes as medical issues rooted in the disease of addiction.

A structural analysis is one that looks at the cultural and physical institutions, such as families and community configurations, as well as hospitals/clinics, schools, jails, and detention centers, among others, that transform our beliefs into practice. It is a framework for understanding our most complex interactions as individuals because it invites us to look at the systems that adults create to amplify and codify our beliefs. These systems include decision-making tools, which include voter ballots, and policies, which include codes of conduct. Similarly, the tools that institutions and other agencies use to collect data, such as the U.S. Census forms, reflect our values. When I was teaching research methods and public policy in the graduate leadership program at Saint Mary's College of California, I always invited my graduate students to consider how people interact with each other to inform what creates a society *and* to consider the things that they create. For example, while we understand that criminal justice policies are designed by law enforcement agencies and legislative bodies, it is actually the *people* within those organizations who make those policies, based upon their individual and collective understanding of issues. If the legal bench interprets addiction to drugs as a criminal legal issue rather than a health issue, then the law enforcement agencies that serve along the justice continuum will respond accordingly.

When these policies are designed without input from the communities that will be disproportionately impacted by them, there are consequences. What is developed is often devoid of frameworks and definitions that reflect the core values of our democracy, and is informed only by a prevailing consciousness that is harmful to the communities being impacted. For example, the wave of "anti-D.E.I." (diversity, equity, and inclusion) rhetoric during the first fifteen days of Donald Trump's second term as president of the United States in 2025 reflected the harsh and mean-spirited political agenda of a small, conservative faction of policymakers and analysts.[2] Historically marginalized groups such as women and girls of all racial groups, people of color, and those with identities representing religious, gender, and sexual diversity became the scapegoat for anything deemed problematic. Even after a tragic airplane collision with a helicopter in the Washington, D.C., area killed sixty-seven people following President

Trump's elimination of key aviation safety measures—unsubstantiated claims emerged of diversity, specifically "D.E.I hires" producing the conditions for this disaster.[3] A departure from the previous decades of progress across the three branches of government to create systems that acknowledge and respond to the needs of one the world's most culturally and linguistically diverse populations, these efforts led to executive orders and mandates in the public and private sectors that ended practices to sustain equal access to resources. Instead, these efforts—which included a federal funding freeze, immediate deportations, and a repeal of reproductive rights for women and girls—stoked fears and sowed confusion, while further concentrating power in the hands of financial elites and corporations. If we think diversity, equity, and inclusion lower the standard of our nation's systems and/or the quality of our material lives, then we build systems that sustain a structure for that to manifest. What we think of an issue informs what we create as the culture of a society.

It's common to think of policy as out of reach for everyday people but, simply put, *people* make policies. Once I understood that, it became clear that girls would benefit from understanding a structural analysis much earlier in their lives. This would allow them to think critically about how policies impact them, then use that information to protect and promote their well-being in the face of life's adversities. Policies inform practice, as they guide the person taking actions. Once I saw the connection between these practices and their deep, personal, and systemic implications, I realized that my training, research, and advocacy needed to address structural issues more explicitly.

In 2004, I left NCCD and became the executive director of the Discrimination Research Center (DRC), which examined the prevalence of discrimination in the public domain. Using mixed methods, including matched-pair test studies and a deep interrogation of implicit bias, we examined language access at local hospitals; we explored employment practices in large corporations; and we looked at other conditions, such as criminal conviction histories, that inform whether people are treated fairly in society. I later facilitated a transition of the DRC to become the research arm of the Thelton E. Henderson Center for Social Justice at UC Berkeley's Law School, where I would serve as the principal investigator and lead author for a series of reports on the impact of Proposition 209 (California's anti–affirmative action legislation). Proposition 209, called the California Civil Rights Initiative, ended affirmative action in public education, contracting, and employment.[4] More than a disparity study, which examines the underutilization of businesses owned by people of color or women of all racial groups compared to their relative percentage of the population in a given industry, these reports provided insight on the historical context for the decision-making in public contracts in the state, and evaluated what happens when affirmative action is removed as a tool to engage a diverse pool of candidates.

Free to Compete? Measuring the Impact of Proposition 209 on Minority Business Enterprises reported on the ten-year impact of Proposition 209 on Minority Business Enterprises seeking public contracts in California's transportation construction industry. *A Vision Fulfilled? The Impact of Proposition 209 on Equal Opportunity for Women Business Enterprises* documented the eleven-year impact of Proposition 209 on Women Business Enterprises seeking public contracts in that same industry. Together, these studies shed light on how people of color and women of all racial groups seeking public contracts have fewer opportunities when there is no intentional system in place to encourage accountability measures for equity and inclusion in sectors where they are underrepresented.

One of the most impactful studies that I led at the Henderson Center looked at the impact of a criminal conviction history on women seeking temporary employment in California. As the first participatory study to examine the impact of a criminal conviction history on the employment of women and girls, I wanted to be sure that we did more than just collect numbers. I wanted to look at the systems—or structures—that impact decision-making for women and girls. I designed it as a participatory study, which meant that formerly incarcerated women, girls, along with people who advocated for their well-being served as a committee to help design the research instruments and interpret the findings of the study. Not only were they an integral part of constructing the research itself, they were also deeply involved in shaping the report. This meant that as a team, we were able to identify and distinguish between the elements of their experiences that were about individual interactions, and those that were about policies and practices. In many ways, this experience allowed us to determine not only the specific places where discriminatory practices were taking place, but where these barriers generated ripples of additional harm in their lives. Ultimately, the study produced the 2008 report that we titled "A Higher Hurdle: Barriers to Employment for Formerly Incarcerated Women."[5]

The report examined how temporary employment agencies responded to the presence or suggestion of a criminal conviction history for women and girls from the age of sixteen. The report revealed that a criminal conviction history poses a specific threat to employment for women and girls of color. The report also provided empirical data that informed advocacy efforts statewide to restrict employers from asking applicants about their criminal conviction history unless it was absolutely necessary. Typically, this question was posed in the form of a box that applicants had to check, to disclose—in a host of arbitrary ways—whether they ever had any contact with the criminal legal system, from arrest to incarceration. This campaign, called "Ban the Box," was championed by several nonprofit agencies, particularly those comprising formerly incarcerated people. All of Us or None, a powerful organization in California led by formerly incarcerated people that advocates "for the rights of formerly—and currently incarcerated people and [their] families," was the primary organization leading the campaign.[6] We joined in partnership with legal advocates and others who wanted to ensure that all people, especially those trying to recover from a criminal conviction history and prevent recidivism, had an opportunity to work with dignity. I loved the opportunity to seek work with people such as Susan Burton, Founder of A New Way of Life Reentry Project; Hamdiya Cooks from Legal Services for Prisoners with Children; Marlene Sanchez, who was leading what was then called the Center for Young Women's Development (it was later renamed the Young Women's Freedom Center); legal advocate and scholar Cynthia Chandler; and other leaders of organizations that were dedicated to ensuring that women and girls were not left behind in conversations about employment equity. This was important work, and it mattered that we were supporting the efforts of organizations that needed data to inform their advocacy. It also mattered that we engaged them throughout the process. It has always been important to me that people involved in research projects are considered more than simply "subjects." They are participants in important work and help those leading formal research inquiries learn about phenomena in specific and dynamic ways, particularly in terms of impact and lived experience. For example, during one of my focus groups with women in Long Beach, I asked about their experiences filling out applications for employment. One woman who had been relatively quiet during the conversation let out a frustrated grunt.

"I get to that question and I just freeze," she said. "I don't keep going."

"I only apply to jobs where people don't ask. . . . I've applied to over two hundred jobs and got three calls back," said another participant. "They'll tell you if they're going to do a background check, and I don't apply to those jobs. I don't want to deal with that. About half of the jobs listed will do a background check, and I don't apply to those jobs a hundred percent of the time."

It was heartbreaking.

But that let me know that this was bigger than just collecting data to record and analyze responses to an arbitrary and discriminatory policy that clipped opportunity for people before they could even get started. It was also about how these policies exacerbate existing personal pain such as rejection, neglect, and the mark of disposability that these women and girls had been negotiating all of their lives. Yes, these women and girls were making decisions as individuals within the context of routine discrimination and bias, but the responses to them were focused *only* on their responses to the victimization, not on the structures that perpetuate it. Over 90 percent of women and girls in the justice system have been subjected to physical, mental, and emotional violence. In this case, women and girls as young as sixteen years old were trying to keep from having to check a box that unnecessarily punishes them for making decisions based upon their own victimization.

Though it wasn't discussed much in the public domain, one of the most important findings of the report is that Black women and girls experienced greater challenges than other women and girls when seeking temporary employment in California. There was an *assumption of criminality* that followed Black women and girls—*whether they had an actual conviction history or not*—which shaped the perception of employers, and thus the employment outcomes for these women and girls. I recognized this phenomenon as one of the most direct interplays between structural policies and individual biases shaping the experiences of women and girls seeking employment. So I knew that I would have to eventually look at how we got here. I would later explore this phenomenon more explicitly in my research and writing on countering the criminalization of Black girls in schools, but at this time it was a signal for me that society must both understand the specific *lived experiences* of people and understand them in the greater context of systems and institutions that reflect the prevailing public consciousness. To understand the full complexity of an issue, it is not enough to look just at numerical data. A thorough analysis of a problem—and its remedies—must also involve the perspectives of those living with the problem. It is a common phrase in advocacy communities that the people closest to the problems are closest to the solutions. Participatory processes that involve those with lived experience of the topic of inquiry adds to the rigor of understanding. It was an essential element of my research and advocacy on this topic.

This study, alongside the study by sociologist Devah Pager, which focused on the experiences of men with a criminal conviction history seeking employment, laid the foundation for the effort I would help to lead at the national office for the NAACP, where I served as the vice president for Research, Advocacy and Economic Programs. In that capacity, I worked alongside then-president Benjamin T. Jealous and then–executive vice president Steven Hawkins to build a programs team that would inform the advocacy of branches throughout the country on education, criminal justice, health, climate justice, and economics. My research on how women and girls were treated when they tried to get a job, in concert with the emergent work of scholar advocates interrogating the reach and disproportionate impact of the criminal legal system on the lives of Black people—and other people of color—was foundational to getting major corporations to stop asking the question about a person's criminal conviction history until absolutely necessary. It wasn't enough to simply have the data from large databases showing recidivism among unemployed or underemployed teens. It was also important to provide a context for the creation of the "box" and why it was discriminatory in the first place. Only then would we be able to shape arguments for inclusion and fair access to employment.

Structures reinforce society's beliefs. If we believe as a society that education is important, we create quality schools. If we believe that people should have their ailments treated by medical professionals, we create well-resourced healing spaces. If we believe that all people deserve an opportunity to access quality food, we pass laws and design spatial plans to locate grocery stores, gardens, and farmers markets in all communities, rather than only in high-net-worth neighborhoods. On the contrary, if we believe that some neighborhoods do not need quality, healthy foods available to them, then we will instead license and zone for more liquor stores. If we believe that addiction is a criminal issue and not a health issue, we will arrest and prosecute people struggling with this disease. The list goes on.

People make policies. People engage in practices. People build institutions. People design, implement, enforce, and replicate the systems that we commonly refer to as "structures of society." For example, the U.S. Census is a structure. It is a system of collecting population data in a uniform manner and is reported using categories that inform the public about the nation's demographics. However, *people* design the census surveys that are distributed across the country, and *people* determine the categories for which data are collected. These categories shift according to the consciousness of their designer(s). When people are trying to make sense of their lives, they often have only their individual experiences to rely on. But it is important for us to teach our girls not to lean *only* into their individual experiences. They must also understand their experiences in context. This is how we activate their sense of knowing such that it grows into critical *thinking*, and then, ultimately, critical *analysis*. That analysis can then determine whether existing structures work in the best interest of girls; and if not, we can seed policies and practices that do. When adults protect the civil rights of girls, we are protecting their collective rights to equal justice under the law. When we challenge the policies and rules that produce inequity in the lives of girls, we are actively dismantling the structures—seen and unseen—that prevent girls from accessing these civil rights.

The National Association of Commissions for Women functions to "sustain, strengthen and advocate for women's commissions in their work to promote equality and justice for all women and girls and ensure they are represented and empowered in their communities," and serves as a coordinating body for state and local commissions on the status of women and girls.[7] While the number of local commissions is currently unknown, most explicitly name "women" or couple "women and girls" in their advocacy. In the early twentieth century, Mary McLeod Bethune and other feminist activists worked at the federal level with president Franklin D. Roosevelt's administration to advise on civil rights matters, engaging an intersectional lens. Since then, efforts have been ongoing to monitor progress among women's affairs. In the 1960s, the Federal Women's Program was established by president Lyndon B. Johnson to advance equality and bar discrimination against women in employment. President William J. Clinton established the President's Interagency Council on Women, for which Hillary Clinton served as honorary chair, in 1995, to address the needs of women across a spectrum of issues, including mentorship, incarceration, rural living, and trafficking, among other concerns. In 2009, President Barack Obama created the White House Council on Women and Girls to "ensure that each of the agencies in which they're charged takes into account the needs of women and girls in the policies they draft, the programs they create, the legislation they support and that the true purpose of our government is to ensure that in America, all things are still possible for all people."[8] Building on the Democratic party's legacy of leveraging White House resources to examine the well-being of women and girls domestically and abroad, President Joseph R. Biden Jr. established the Gender Policy Council (GPC) in 2020 and launched the first-ever National Strategy on Gender Equity and Equality. The council worked to "advance gender equity and equality in both domestic and foreign policy development and implementation. The GPC covered a range of issues—including economic security, health, gender-based violence and education—with a focus on gender equity and equality, and particular attention to the barriers faced by women and girls" at the intersections of their identities.[9] This body was a primary liaison between the White House and the leaders of large women- and girls-centered organizations. It was also an important co-convenor of high-level discussions about systemic issues impacting girls across the nation. Importantly, they engaged an interagency model to advance in ten specific priority areas, including improving economic security and accelerating economic growth; eliminating gender-based violence; ensuring equal opportunity and equity in education; advancing gender equity and fairness in the justice and immigration systems; and promoting gender equity in mitigating and responding to climate change, among others.[10]

Councils and associations like these are important and can help to increase visibility and access for girls across federal agencies. For example, the Philadelphia Commission on Women, a ten-member body in Pennsylvania established by the Mayor's Office of Engagement for Women, has the express mission to "improve lives of Philadelphia's women, girls, and individuals who identify as female." The commission focuses on wage equity, education, gender-based violence, and entrepreneurship, among other issues. In 2019, the commission hosted a "Teen Dating Violence, Sexual Assault, and Healthy Decision Making" workshop for girls enrolled in the Ambitious Queens Uniquely Identified for Rising to be Educated (AQUIRE), an affinity group at Furness High School, and in the Women of Tomorrow program, an affinity group at the Academy at Palumbo High School.[11] These commissions are only as strong as the advocacy for their existence.

Dismantling the structural barriers to girls' success requires going beyond simply establishing an oversight and/or advocacy body such as a commission. It requires adults in leadership positions to use our resources to deploy the actions, items, strategies, and people that we know to create equal opportunity for girls. This means conducting audits of existing policies and practices and revising them with the well-being of girls as a specific goal. Our goal, as adults who are committed to the well-being of our girls, is to support their development as community leaders with an inclusive and capacious worldview. When we partner with girls to do these things, we increase their capacity to grow advocacy from within the structures we create with them, rather than trying to bang down the door from outside. *Justice* for girls is inherently structural, and its realization depends on the extent to which we invest in their ability to build political power.

Girls for Gender Equity (GGE), a New York–based nonprofit whose mission is to "work intergenerationally, through a Black feminist lens, to center the leadership of Black girls and gender-expansive young people of color in reshaping culture and policy through advocacy, youth-centered programming, and narrative shift to achieve gender and racial justice,"[12] has demonstrated that its mission is not only achievable, but effective in building out the type of leadership that we want our girls to embody. Social worker and activist Joanne N. Smith, the organization's founder and CEO, and I have been working to advance girls' life outcomes for decades. We have organized and participated in local town halls about the well-being of girls. We have testified together before the

Congressional Caucus on Black Women and Girls about school-based disciplinary disparities, and Joanne has been a long-standing supporter of the federal, state, and local legislation seeking political and structural remedies to the harm that girls experience at the intersections of their identities.

Teaching girls about how organizations work prepares them for leadership of these organizations. To withhold information about how structures operate hinders their ability to weigh in on the very ideas and actions that limit them, and impacts their well-being in other ways. One day in 2024, Joanne and I sat down to talk about why teaching girls about structures is an essential investment.

"Girls have to understand how systems and policies work. So, it's extremely important to GGE that a lot of education happens," Joanne said. "Our curriculum includes modules to understand government, civic engagement, and the voting process. Teaching them about structures helps them understand the matrix and what is happening to them. For young people, making meaning of the conditions that produce harm—or safety—in their lives is empowering. If I'm between a rock and a hard place and I bang my head on a rock, and then you tell me that I caused my own damage, that's a problem. You have to help get me out of there, then ask, How did I get here? And once I know the answer, how do I then get in a position to acquire and maintain power to create access to opportunities that allow me to thrive and grow into what I ideally want to be?"

Engaging girls in the structural change of their communities is a specific skill. It begins with education and conversation, but also involves listening (without judgment) to what girls say about the structures—physical, institutional, and/or policy-based—that impact their lives. This is the foundation for a girl-centered approach to the cultivation of a critical analysis.

"Every single structure that Black girls are a part of often does not inherently work in their favor, because most of these structures are not designed for them," Joanne said, clearing her throat.

A girl-centered approach is one that is intentionally designed to respond to the needs of girls. The design reflects an infrastructure of support, with staffing and design of the physical space, that takes into consideration the specific experiences that impact girls' well-being. These approaches recognize the inherent intersectionality of girls' lives—as young people who are female and youth at once, alongside their other identities (such as sexuality, ability, class, and so on) that inform their experiences with people, institutions, and policies.

"From my work in social work, addressing the HIV and AIDS crisis among families impacted by poverty, to my work in schools, the framework of equity was never lost on me," Joanne continued. "Within every systemic problem, every structural problem, we tend to only see children as *collateral,* as opposed to putting them at the center."

Equity is the enactment of policies or practices that bring justice to a group that is experiencing harm. Equality is about treating everyone the same without regard for circumstance. Equity is about doing what's right to give everyone a fair opportunity. With an equity frame, girls emerge as more than collateral, because they are at the center of efforts to make life outcomes more just. The decisions that policymakers and organizational leaders advance through an equity lens are outcome driven, rather than merely symbolic.

Joanne continued, "It was very clear, very early on, that however we were going to address issues as an organization, we would have to get to the *root* of the root. Sometimes it's *dismantling,* or consciously and systemically operating on and pulling apart systems. But sometimes you have to destroy systems and structures that really are doing more harm than good, with the anticipation that you're building something different."

I agree. Dismantling the systems that produce barriers to girls' success means that we have to first identify what those structures are. Then we determine the best course of action. We have to look at them, describe them, and interrogate them, in order to move toward the goal of creating something better. This is the work of moving from destruction and deconstruction to production.

"It can't just be about what you believe about girls," she continued. "It also has to be about facilitating access to greater opportunities. We knew that in order to do that, we had to shift 'hearts and minds.' That's a cultural narrative shift. They had to share stories and write new narratives that were centering girls' voices."

Joanne and Girls for Gender Equity were critical partners with Kimberlé Crenshaw's African American Policy Forum on the initial #WhyWeCantWait campaign in 2014, which challenged the rhetoric of racial justice movements that sought to prioritize only the conditions of men and boys of color. The #WhyWeCantWait campaign was a multimedia organizing effort to share the urgent issues facing Black girls, to increase public awareness, and to generate public interest in remedies to these problems. Joanne, GGE, and the African American Policy Forum led efforts to organize *Breaking Silence,* a town hall hearing on girls of color.[13] *Breaking Silence* addressed five key issues:

1. Gender-Specific Burdens (i.e., Teenage Pregnancy, Caregiving)
2. Foster Care and Aging Out of Care
3. Human Trafficking of Commercially Sexually Exploited Children
4. School Pushout and Criminalization (in schools)
5. Criminalization (in general) and Incarceration

As a result of the organizing strategy, GGE led a citywide effort in NYC to center the well-being of our girls and gender expansive youth called the Young Women's Initiative. This partnership between the New York City Council, philanthropy, and girls-serving organizations throughout the city produced work groups and other strategic planning sessions, which led to the development of a substantial series of partnerships and recommendations to the benefit of the young people, shared in the publication "NYC Young Women's Initiative Report and Recommendations."[14] GGE continued listening sessions and school-based interventions in NYC for the overuse of exclusionary discipline, which are the disciplinary responses to students that remove them from their learning or school (suspensions, expulsions, etc.). Through participatory action research, they published *The School Girls Deserve: Youth-Driven Solutions for Creating Safe, Holistic, and Affirming New York City Public Schools*.[15] Their work did not end there. They continue to advance discussions about Title IX and the need for every school to enforce existing laws designed to protect girls' well-being and to produce convening spaces for a policy agenda for Black girls.

"The Young Women's Initiative was a beautiful coming together of the right people at the right time in New York City," Joanne said. "By the end of this cross-sector effort of youth organizations, government, philanthropy, and research, we committed to have a declaration for young people, girls, and trans young people of color. We wanted it to be accompanied by a commitment of resources from government and philanthropy, and it was able to grow because philanthropy was a huge part of that effort. The New York Women's Foundation and other women's foundations were able to say, '*Oh yeah, we want this in our state, too, and we will support it.*' GGE provided technical assistance for eight other community-based organizations that hosted young women's advisory councils throughout the nation. It all worked, because working with young people isn't just having them in the room. It's a craft, an art, and a practice. It's a program, and it's work."

Joanne is right. Teaching girls about dismantling structural barriers that disrupt or undermine their development is about more than just having them in the room. I recognized that during my juvenile justice work in Louisiana. Presence alone is merely symbolic when the room is not prepared to receive them. To be transformational, to be unlimited, girls and young women must be in positions of leadership and influence. The foundations of this influence are in the recognition of basic rights. GGE understood that and launched a major effort to co-construct the Black Girl Bill of Rights, a policy agenda that would reflect the importance not only of naming girls, but of engaging them in its creation.

"The Black Girl Bill of Rights was so beautifully developed by the young people," Joanne said. "It was really their declaration of humanity, of freedom, of writing themselves into history in a way that allows them to demand the space that they were constantly being told was *not* for them, or that they had to wait for."

Between 2009 and 2016, public discourse about youth impacted by racial injustice overwhelmingly focused on the conditions of boys of color. The tragic killings of seventeen-year-old Trayvon Martin in 2012, who was murdered by neighborhood patrol volunteer George Zimmerman in Florida; twelve-year-old Tamir Rice, who was killed in 2014 in Ohio by a police officer who mistook his toy gun for a real one; and other boys killed by police or extensions of state violence, fixed in the public consciousness that boys were the primary group impacted by the failures of public safety. A cacophony of protests around the country led to the rapid growth of the Black Lives Matter movement, and to an explosion of investments—in time, education, and financial resources—in the well-being of Black boys and other boys of color. A major funder collaborative that included foundations and philanthropic intermediaries mobilized foundation support for men and boys' programming across a spectrum of issues (such as education, employment, and youth development, among others) that resulted in steady growth in the mid-2010s—from $50.9 million in 2013 to $62.7 million in 2014.[16] Boys were being rapidly organized on school campuses to participate in gender-responsive programming, with rallying cries made across civil rights and social justice spaces to center on boys' issues as the primary strategy to achieve community well-being.

Women and men worked together across sectors, formally and informally, organizing to direct their resources and attention to the very dire needs of boys. Women in politics locked in on the message that the primary pathway to improving racial conditions was by improving the conditions of boys and young men. In 2016, the New York City Black Male Donor Collaborative and the Young Men's Initiative—efforts launched by Mayor Michael Bloomberg in 2011 to address racial disparities affecting young men and boys in health, education, enrichment, and employment—committed $27 million, complementing a three-year private investment of $60 million to address these needs in the city.[17] The California Funders for Men and Boys of Color—a network of CEOs from philanthropic organizations throughout the state—mobilized more than $500,000 in "seed grants," funding that supported emergent ideas and programs in the early stages of their development, to support innovative interventions for boys.[18] Between 2015 and 2019, they mobilized more than $149 million annually to "support better outcomes for boys and men of color and remove barriers to opportunity."[19] These are just two of many examples of robust financial investments in boys that emerged across the country. Scholars produced original research papers across disciplines, including economics, law, education, and others, demonstrating the great disparities faced by boys and young men of color, and public agencies shared information that disaggregated data for one of the first times by race and gender—but only for boys. All of these steps were necessary investments.

The problem was that leaders in government, advocacy, and philanthropy interpreted this focus on boys as an excuse to ignore or undermine the needs of girls, many of whom were experiencing similar conditions in their homes, schools, and communities. When Kimberlé Crenshaw and I asked public agencies such as the U.S. Department of Education for data about girls at the time, disaggregated to also show trends for girls by racial identity, for example, we were initially met with the same response: no. We asked why, pointing out that if data about boys were available, they must also be available for girls, but this logic didn't initially compel the public agencies to share data with us. On more than one occasion, leaders in philanthropy told me that our efforts to explore the conditions of girls were "not a priority," since girls' issues were not as urgent as the boys' needs. But I have always believed that our collective liberation rests on the widespread ability to include a robust gender analysis in racial justice work, and vice versa.

"It was a time when the world was actively erasing what Black and Brown girls in particular go through, because there was a way in which the media was uplifting that only Black and Brown boys go through it," Joanne continued. "Every structural institution, from schools to the federal government, were centering only Black and Brown boys. So the Black Girl Bill of Rights was a way for Black girls to demand rights and autonomy. They renamed it *Black Girls Declaration of Freedom and Humanity*. It was their way of saying that they deserve this space, and don't have to make themselves small to enter the space."

The sting of being told to "wait your turn" or "you're not a priority" as you suffer under the same conditions for which others receive help is a special kind of torture. Our girls were sharing the same schools, the same families, the same faith-based institutions, the same hospitals and clinics, the same increased surveillance from the presence of law enforcement in schools, and the same employment landscape as their male counterparts. While, of course, their experiences were different, as informed by gender, the thematic dehumanization experienced by Black children and other children of color at the hand of these institutions was shared. To combat the erasure of girls in public discourses on safety and child welfare in particular, a growing number of women began to partner in ways that could create an echo chamber for demands. Like the Women's Movement of the 1960s and 1970s, the goal of this social movement is equity. Only this time, the call isn't just for us as women. It is for our *girls.* It is for our younger selves.

"Within every institution, Black girls especially were told, 'Well, you're *here,* but it doesn't matter.'" Joanne frowned, shook her head, and continued. "Why? Why is this happening to you? Most of the girls who are here have helped shape even the work for boys. Black girls are always actively advocating for their brothers and men. So it was a moment for us to declare their freedom and humanity, and to have them shape what that means. As adults, we can always declare something and develop a space and condition for young people. With the Black Girl Bill of Rights, we partnered with advocates, including A Long Walk Home, and scholars to create a huge conference, the Black Girl Movement Conference at Columbia University. Our Sisters in Strength youth organizers were planning to present at that conference, so it started there."

Sisters in Strength (SIS) is a program of Girls for Gender Equity. It began as a two-year program for teen cisgender and transgender girls entering the tenth or eleventh grades focused on providing education and training for involvement in social justice efforts. Its programming evolved over the years to include a specific focus on surviving sexual violence. Today, SIS is described as a "survivor circle for youth survivors of childhood sexual abuse and their allies."[20] Like SIS, A Long Walk Home, a national nonprofit organization based in Chicago, Ilinois, engages adolescent girls in creative expressions to heal from sexual violence.

"Within the framework of the Black Girl Movement Conference, they asked, what is the movement that we want to see?"

Joanne continued. "Then the idea of a Black Girl Bill of Rights came up. As the girls were talking about it, they wanted to include more of their sisters. They wanted to include the voices of those who were there at the conference in New York, knowing there'll be hundreds of girls there. And so, they created a very beautiful, long scroll of paper and laid it out within the room and set up a workshop. They talked to the other people about how when the U.S. Constitution was created, they were not considered in its development."

Major policies in the U.S. are rarely created with girls in mind. Even those that seek to protect the rights of women do not plainly consider what girls might need. While girls are theoretically protected under many of the amendments in the Bill of Rights of the U.S. Constitution, their specific needs are not named explicitly.

"What is it for us to be realized and free?" Joanne asked, pausing to reflect on the beauty of young people who had convened in Harlem for the conference, entering and exiting the room where the development of this Black Girl Bill of Rights was being crafted.

Ultimately, the Black Girl Bill of Rights—called the Black Girls Declaration of Freedom and Humanity—is held by GGE's advocacy through the National Agenda for Black Girls. It includes a focus on six key policy areas, and includes the "right to education and information about African and Black history" and "the right to real sex education, contraception, tampons, and pads." (The full text of the Black Girl Bill of Rights is shared in Appendix A.) I remember taking that document with me in draft form to different cities around the United States, from Philadelphia to Columbus to New Orleans to San Antonio to Los Angeles. I visited more than thirty cities over the course of eighteen months and shared a version of the Black Girl Bill of Rights with girls and young women from elementary school to college age, in each city.

"This is what girls are creating in New York," I'd say. "What do you think?"

Almost immediately, hands would shoot into the air, murmurs would fill the room, and girls would take advantage of the opportunity to add to the document and discuss its existing elements. Girls would start chatting with each other and sharing some of their ideas with me. Adults in the room sometimes took note of the specific issues girls would raise that were unique to their school or community, so that even if they did not make it to the final iteration of the Bill of Rights document, these concerns would not be lost. Those small activities engendered trust, which then led girls to feel even safer in sharing their thoughts. The positive energy around the document was always so palpable. This was largely because the act of co-constructing the document became an exercise in which the girls were able to apply their *knowing*. They were able to activate their wisdom. Girls were at the center of a policy discussion, and they reveled in it.

"What was always striking to me was that the Bill of Rights included not just conversations about policies," I said to Joanne. "It was also about free access to tampons and other feminine hygiene products. It was about play! That really struck me because I was like, wow, what structural barriers are keeping our girls from *playing*? They were framing these things that we assume are a natural part of childhood, as a constitutional right that they were not experiencing. It was in your face. It was plain."

"It was," Joanne responded. "I was proud of them for elevating that, and bringing that to the attention of many adults who were not really tapped in. That right to play was so beautiful, because it was the youngest person in the room at the time who could write, who added 'play' to the Black Girl Bill of Rights. And everybody was like, *Oh, yeah!* It didn't matter your age. We were all connecting our right to be free and to have fun."

Joanne and I both played basketball as girls—she in New York and I in California. I remember my own journey of carrying a basketball around with me all the time in case I found a court to play on. In my neighborhood, gangs and the proliferation of drugs had begun to shape the landscape of play, especially for me as a girl who played ball with other girls but also with boys. Once I went to play basketball at the gym down the street from my home and when I knocked on the door, a man answered it.

He looked at me, standing there with my basketball under my arm, and asked, "You really play basketball?"

"Yeah," I said with certainty. I thought he was challenging me to prove my skills. "Then you can't come in here," he said. He redirected me to an outdoor court around the corner and up the hill.

The gym was used for illicit activities, and he knew I just wanted to play. So he sent me somewhere else. Sometimes the community will protect girls in this way, but often they do not.

"The safety of girls is always a consideration, even for those like me and you who were brave enough to play," Joanne continued. "What we experienced while playing, if men and boys were playing, or if men and boys or folks were in the crowd, is people calling us names or threatening us, questioning our femininity, our humanity and our abilities. This has hindered many, but the right to play has become a key component of our National Agenda for Black Girls because they will never erase our joy."

Advocacy for structures that advance the well-being of our girls is an investment in their liberated futures. Despite how we might feel when we hear the word, "structures" are not too big for us to influence. As with the National Agenda for Black Girls, girls are examining "big" issues—structures—in real time, so as adults, we should be able to do the same. This starts by addressing how some of the common questions we get in advocacy work on behalf of girls can expand beyond just being reflective of "gender-responsive" rhetoric for girls: How do we assess a policy or law for its gender-responsiveness? How do we measure an institution for its gender-responsiveness? How do we support girls' limitless possibility by turning "gender-responsive" language into an actual investment in them?

How to Assess a Policy for Gender-Responsiveness for Girls

Policies are frameworks for action. To assess whether a given policy is in service to the unlimited, liberated futures of girls, we must begin by asking questions about the intent of the policy, and whether there is an impact on girls. Once it has been established whether there is an impact on girls, then we can move into a more specific set of questions.

1. *Does the policy name its impact—or intended impact—on girls explicitly?*
   There are many facially gender-neutral policies—written and unwritten—that impact girls; but without an explicit mention of girls as a population being considered by the policy, there is a risk of their erasure in the measures used to determine programmatic success. Determine if it acknowledges their existence, explicitly or by proxy, or if it intends to have an impact without respect to the age, gender, or other identities potentially impacted by the policy. It's important not to assume that because girls aren't explicitly named in a policy, that they will not be impacted by it. Taking consideration of how dress code policies, for example, will impact girls is important when designing codes of conduct in schools. Facially gender-neutral policies, such as referrals to restorative approaches in schools, are often more difficult to address because they present an illusion of parity or fairness that

may not exist. In this scenario, while a school's referral process to a restorative program may not consider gender, the actions taken by girls may not be considered eligible ("qualifying offenses") for participation in the program. Does the policy lead to undesired outcomes, even if it is facially gender neutral? For example, how are girls being served by the restorative program? What are the girls' outcomes in the program? Is the program suited to respond to their needs?

2. *Does the policy uplift or undermine girls' well-being?* It seems like a no-brainer. After determining whether girls are named in the policy, we need to ensure there are ways to measure the policy's specific impact on girls. What data points need to be collected and monitored in order to determine impact? It is most effective to explore this in partnership with girls. Create spaces for girls to be a part of the conversation about policies' impact on their lives. All conversations don't have to be a critique. Also invite girls to use "Appreciative Inquiry"—or the centering of an unconditional positive question—when they are exploring the impact of policy.

    Appreciative Inquiry is associated with the family of Action Research Methods, which blends quantitative and qualitative research with practice to address an issue using a cyclical engagement model that includes planning, action, observation, and reflection.[21] As a research method, Appreciative Inquiry uses quantitative and qualitative ethnographic research methods including interviews, document analysis, participant observation, etc., but prioritizes unconditional positive questions. An appreciative inquiry is one that focuses on what works to remedy an issue or problem and builds from these discoveries to generate positive outcomes.

For example, if girls are brought in to examine the impact of a policy on language access at local health clinics, instead of just asking, "How has this policy been an issue for you?" or "How have you been impacted by this policy?" You may consider: "How does this policy miss an opportunity to expand your health and well-being?" "What are ways that language access, when provided thoughtfully, and with care, can improve your life?" "What does thoughtful care look like to you?" This approach invites us to imagine the positive alternatives to a crisis or issue and activates the imaginations of our girls in the construction of its reality.

3. *Is the policy or program culturally competent?*
A policy or program is not gender-responsive if it's not culturally competent, and vice versa. In order to measure the full extent of a policy or program's competencies, we must first understand the numerous cultures and identities that girls hold. No one girl is exactly the same as another; but there are some shared experiences that can help to assess whether a policy's impact accounts for cultural differences. The healthcare and treatment industry has undertaken a long-standing conversation about the importance of culturally competent care, from the initial point of patient access to healthcare professionals, to communications regarding community-based prevention and intervention opportunities. Often missing is the inclusion of a youthful perspective on these matters, particularly those having to do with cultural

interpretations that impact feminine healthcare. For example, traditional measures of optimal weight are informed by cultural norms and behaviors. While the weight index for obesity might be a BMI of 30 or higher, cultural preferences regarding the distribution of the weight might elevate a standard of beauty that embraces a thicker body type—as a symbol of both wealth (where thin bodies are associated with poverty and malnourishment) and beauty. So if a young woman is called "thick" by her peers, she may receive it as a compliment. As American poet Lucille Clifton wrote in an homage to her hips, "these hips are big hips / they need space to / move around in. / they don't fit into little / petty places. these hips / are free hips. / they don't like to be held back. / these hips have never been enslaved . . ."[22] These reflections matter when exploring interpretation of policy and access to care.

4. *What does the leadership of the institution that created the policy or program look like?*
   Determine the composition of the institution's leadership—from most junior to most senior—and map if it reflects an intersectional framework when responding to the communities of girls being served. If there is no leadership reflective of the community being serviced, then what actually informs the existing leadership's understanding of the issue? A learning institution is one that engages opportunities for growth at every level. Dismantling structures requires coordination, community, and connections to decision-makers associated with the issue and its implementation. Girls need access to that, as do the adults who will elevate their perspectives. Possible

questions to ask include: Are the hours, programming, and services designed to consider the specific needs of girls? Were they part of designing it? Is the leadership of girls factored into aspects of services rendered by this organization?

We expand "gender-responsive" language to become actual investments in our girls by doing more than just asking the questions. As Joanne shared, we must also develop an infrastructure of support that measures impact and establishes systems of accountability. We must check for alignment between mission, priorities, and budget allocations and determine if the budget speaks to our values. Finally, we must create spaces for girls to exercise organizational leadership—and design a system to grow and support this leadership.

The infrastructure adults build for girls is what breathes life into Joanne's invitation for adults raising and working with girls to do more than just bring them into a room. The time and resources we use to dismantle structures that cause girls harm must be participatory, by including them, and they must be intersectional, by responding to girls across their identities. This is how the everyday actions of adults working with girls move from being "gender-responsive," which acknowledges their existence in response strategies, to being "transformative," which means the actions result in new manifestations of becoming.

Edna Branch Jackson is the former mayor of Savannah, Georgia, becoming the first Black woman to hold that position in 2012. A celebrated figure in the civil rights movement in Savannah, she has served as an educator and mentor to many of the city's leading political and scholarly figures currently. One day, I had the honor of listening to her recount some of her journey as a public servant during the city's StoryCon, a convening of storytellers who come together to share powerful stories of the human experience. In conversation with my friend Bertice Berry, she spoke of her experiences as a young activist using her body—and mind—to fight racial segregation. Sitting with humility and laughing, she quietly dropped valuable insights into the thinking of young people who were the heart of the modern civil rights movement of the 1960s. She described how it felt to be in community with other young people fighting for racial justice, and how they worked collectively to examine laws, policies, and practices that were causing harm to them and their communities. Understanding that their freedom was sometimes contingent upon their willingness to be arrested and jailed for violating the current laws, she shared that nothing—nothing—was a matter of happenstance.

"Before I be a slave, I'll be buried in my grace and with my Lord, I'll be free," she sang, revisiting the songs she and her fellow protesters sang when they were arrested for trying to integrate a public beach. An active activist for racial justice, Mayor Jackson told story after story of challenging discriminatory laws and practices that kept her from enjoying the freedoms of her White counterparts. In all, not only did she help to end segregation of beaches, she also helped to desegregate public schools and public eating spaces. Credited with bringing the first integrated group to the 1963 March on Washington, Mayor Jackson described how families worked together to use their homes as collateral to bail protesters arrested for challenging racial discrimination out of jail.

"It was a strategy," she said.

I marveled at her courage and was eager to know more about what was given to her as a girl that fed this fighting spirit dismantling structural barriers to equity.

"What investments were made in you as a girl that you think are important to pay forward?" I asked her.

She looked at me and nodded, pausing for a moment to consider her response.

"People wanted me to be successful," she finally responded. "I try to mentor people. To this day, people say, if you want to run for public office, see Mayor Edna. Let young folks know that you want them to succeed."

The greatest infrastructure adults can build for our girls is one that supports the pursuit of their unbridled freedom through a network of mentors and institutions that nourishes their courage to be their full selves in exercising their *knowing* and discovering and then actualizing their purpose. To secure successful outcomes for our girls, we must invest in a collective effort to keep their bodies safe along the way.

4

PROTECT GIRLS FROM GENDER-BASED VIOLENCE

You don't have to be anyone but yourself to be worthy.
—Tarana Burke, founder of the #metoo movement

In 2023, I was a guest presenter for a youth business and leadership summit outside Sydney, Australia. The summit was designed to engage about a hundred young people across the gender spectrum in conversations about mind-set development, decision-making, and other skills associated with entering the workforce or exploring entrepreneurship. I talked about *Charisma's Turn,* and shared some of my own experiences and lessons growing up in the United States. For the larger group, I stared into the faces of young people as I talked through the concept of perseverance. I shared that early in my life, I was not allowed to say "I can't," a phrase my mother disallowed and treated as a curse word. The students all listened attentively as I encouraged them to overcome the temptation to quit before they even get started—to say "I can't" before they even try to accomplish something. Later, for a breakout session, I had the opportunity to connect with just the girls. The large multipurpose room was arranged for girls to have a private place to discuss issues of specific importance to them. A lineup of presenters offered advice to the girls about ways to navigate everything from sexism and misogyny in advertising to the fundamentals of entrepreneurship. I wanted to build on a topic I had offered earlier in the week about the importance of believing in oneself even when others think success is not possible, but along the way, I realized that the girls were asking questions that suggested they wanted a deeper conversation.

I paced the stage to make eye contact with as many of the girls as I could. The diverse crowd of girls, which was made up mostly of girls of European descent, but also included girls of Indigenous Australian, Asian, African, and South American ancestry, stared back at me with interest. I imagine part of what made me compelling to them was the foreign mark of my American accent. But I also recognized that I was offering them an opportunity to discuss something real, in a safe space.

"Show of hands," I asked at some point in our intimate discussion. "How many of you have experienced, or know someone who has experienced, sexual violence?"

Every hand in the room went up. Every single hand.

We went on to talk about how significant it is that girls are united in the fight against sexual violence, and the types of investments they want and need to keep them safe. Many of the girls offered specific examples of how they could be safer in their communities—offering self-defense mechanisms that ranged from physical to emotional support. Others stared at me silently or nodded in agreement if our eyes happened to meet. Later that evening, I was sitting at dinner when a girl came up and tapped me on the shoulder.

"Can I talk to you?" she asked. Through her thick Australian accent, my heart registered what my ears may not have readily detected.

I agreed immediately.

We walked over to a quiet area of the cafeteria. I looked down into her soft gray eyes as she ran her hands through her shoulder-length brown hair.

"What happened to you, happened to me," she said.

"I'm so sorry to hear that," I responded. "Were you able to get help?"

"No," she said. "It's happening right *now.*"

Immediately, my heart sank. This was her cry for help. I went into response mode, connecting with the program leadership and calling my friends in sexual assault prevention work back in the States to see if they had relationships with similar organizations in Australia. We spoke for a little while longer, so that I could offer her some survival strategies in real time, but the knowledge that in every audience—always—girls are surviving attacks on their bodies overwhelmed me with dread.

I spend so much time discussing and engaging the topic of sexual violence in my research and advocacy work because it is the underlying vulnerability for girls and women, *the* thing that disproportionately disrupts their ability to walk confidently in their purpose toward a life of limitless possibility. But, while the brave ones almost always seem to be the girls, the onus of responsibility for ensuring that conditions are ripe for their leadership—the cultivation of their power—falls on the rest of us. Sexual violence is one of a few pillars of gender-based violence. The World Health Organization describes any act of violence against women that "results in, or is likely to result in, physical, sexual, or mental harm, or suffering to women, including threats of such acts, coercion, or arbitrary deprivation of liberty, whether occurring in public or in private," as gender-based violence. Sexual violence along with intimate partner violence/domestic violence are core components of a large and long list of assaults that threaten the well-being of women—and of girls, though rarely explicitly named. From the assaults that cause psychological harm, such as verbal abuse and controlling behaviors, to the physical acts of harm that include rape and unwanted touching, among other acts, gender-based violence is the epidemic rarely named in discussions on public health.

This issue is so pervasive that some people, including educators, students, public agency leaders, and other practitioners I have worked with, tend to consider it too big to address. In the early 2000s, I worked with local probation departments in Northern California, helping to facilitate processes for them to address the overrepresentation of youth of color in contact with the juvenile court and criminal legal system. As a consultant I trained probation officers on how to reduce racial disparities among young people across the continuum of decisions that are held within the department. This included decisions at intake, decisions associated with responses to violations, decisions associated with confinement, and decisions associated with placement within institutions upon confinement.

During one of the initial training sessions, a probation officer said to me, "The thing is, none of these disparities are really our fault in probation. We just take in who law enforcement brings to us."

I smiled at him, because I'd heard that one before. Many times, probation officers would absolve themselves of responsibility associated with the disparities present in their system by saying it was the fault of the police.

"I hear you. There are many decisions that you don't make that result in disproportionate representation," I remember saying. "But I want us to focus on the decisions you *do* make."

After we spent more than two hours talking about all of the decisions probation officers make each day, it finally dawned on him that he could make more of an impact than he originally thought he could.

"We don't make the decision to arrest," he finally said. "But if a kid comes in to us, we do make the decision about which bed to place him in . . . and if he gets put in a bed up front, I'm more likely to see if he violates the rules. If he's in the back, I won't see it . . . and I notice that we tend to put the Black and Latino guys in the front."

What this probation officer first thought was an issue too big for him to address—racial disparities across the juvenile justice system—became something that he could actually impact within his sphere of daily decision-making and influence. I have found the same to be true across sectors. When people think of gender-based violence, they often comment about how big an issue it is—but we make decisions regularly that can impact whether and how girls are safe, and how others are educated not to be agents of harm.

Though the U.S. Department of Justice's Office on Violence against Women, between 1994 and 2005, was providing technical assistance and public resources to eradicate gender-based violence, few campaigns have been able to effectively penetrate and neutralize the widespread apathy about this issue like the #metoo movement did. In 2017, actress Alyssa Milano used the hashtag to respond to the sexual violence that was rampant in Hollywood, saying that "she, too" had experienced sexual violence, setting off an explosion of virtual testimonies about people's experiences with sexual violence in other sectors. At the time, it seemed as if everyone I knew—and millions I didn't—had experienced sexual violence like I had. We didn't have to detail every trauma to find connection with each other, or to know that we needed systemic change. Actress Rosario Dawson shared in a 2017 Twitter post, "All too pervasive . . . Me too. #MeToo #TogetherWeRise."[1] She was right about that—gender-based violence is all too pervasive. Scores of actresses and actors shared their experiences with sexual and other gender-based violence followed by the #MeToo hashtag. From celebrities such as Reese Witherspoon, Gabrielle Union, and Terry Crews to the millions of people without public profiles, the hashtag galvanized survivors to speak out against gender-based violence.

What Alyssa did not know was that she was calling in the

life's work of Tarana Burke. Tarana first used and popularized the #metoo framework in 2006, based upon work that began for her in the 1990s to address childhood sexual assault, particularly among Black girls. Immediately, Black women familiar with Tarana's history made sure that social media outlets cited her foundational work. Alyssa embraced Tarana as the founder of the #metoo framework, and a global collective testimony about the shared gender-based violence that women and girls experience was born.

I discussed this journey with Tarana as it pertains to our girls.

"I read your book *Unbound,* and there's so much to pull from your experience about why investing in girls is so necessary," I started.

Unbound chronicled Tarana's devastating story of childhood sexual violence in the Bronx, New York.[2] It highlights a personal journey through sexual violence and its intersections with racialized gender bias, which ultimately leads to transformation, both personal and professional. As I was reading her book, I was struck by the honesty of her youthful vulnerability and of the communities that contributed to her awakening as an activist. As she discussed the cyclical nature of gender-based violence and its erasure in public discourses about the well-being of our youth (especially when harm to young people is done by trusted community leaders), I was reminded of how much gender-based violence is a health issue.

"People don't see sexual and gender-based violence as a health crisis, because we ignore so much about the wellness and health of Black and Brown women and girls in particular," Tarana said. "From a medical perspective, there are direct correlations between trauma and health. We often focus only on the physical act when the violence happens. There's what you experienced as a child, as a teenager, or as an adult—that physical harm—but then there's the extended harm, which is all the stuff that happens *after*. That's what we hold in our bodies and ignore. I say this all the time . . . I don't think people really stop to think about what it means. What we experience at six, seven, eight, or nine years old now lives with you for the rest of your life. That, and the fact that studies show the likelihood of it happening again is exponential, means you are holding multiple traumas in your body, often unaddressed. Then we have to live, work, play, and be educated. We're supposed to live, learn, and worship in the same places where we were harmed—and that brings on another level of psychological torture. We are supposed to show up and operate in the world in particular kinds of ways while holding this trauma and watching people actively not care! There are no resources to address this. There are no campaigns. There are no slogans. There are no commercials or stories being told. This is why resourcing programs and activities addressing violence against women and girls is essential."

The work to support young survivors of gender-based violence is still implemented through small, sporadically placed programs that use multiple modalities and interventions such as therapy, art, education, etc., often without resources. While there are no reliable data on the average annual budget for sexual violence response programs in the United States, which may include direct services, counseling, intermediate housing, or medical responses, it is no secret that these organizations are woefully underfunded. The CDC estimates that the average lifetime cost of one rape is $122,461, which, when multiplied by the 25 million reported cases of rape in the U.S., amounts to more than $3 trillion.[3] According to a 2022 study by scholars at the Johns Hopkins School of Public Health, the annual cost to incarcerate perpetrators of child sexual abuse is $5.4 billion.[4] Their estimates show that the amount U.S. taxpayers spend on prison and Sex Offender Civil Commitment (SOCC) inmates—programs that hold sex offenders indefinitely in custody after they have served a prison sentence—for sex crimes against children is nearly $49 billion, including approximately $33 billion for state prisoners, $5.2 billion for federal prisoners, and $10.7 billion for SOCC inmates.[5] Outside of the costs associated with incarceration, the total economic burden of childhood sexual assault is more than $9.3 billion, when health care, productivity loss, child welfare, violence and crime, special education, and suicide are all considered.[6] But the total expenses of girls and the women who work with survivors of childhood sexual assault in paid and volunteer programs, and who disproportionately experience childhood sexual assault themselves, aren't often considered in such analyses. That's partially what makes Tarana's work so powerful. She's a survivor, and a survivor who works with other survivors. These layers provide insights into what inspires her dedication to girls' well-being.

"You will never make me stop screaming at the top of my lungs for my girls," she said.

It's her *knowing,* and her purpose. Though we know that 1 in 5 girls experiences sexual violence, a 2024 study found that the prevalence of child sexual abuse has increased due to the access provided by the internet. When online sexual abuse is factored in, the rate of child sexual abuse increases to nearly 32 percent for girls (and nearly 11 percent for boys).[7] Making matters worse is that media coverage of child sexual assault is also complicated and undertheorized. A 2011 comprehensive study conducted by the Berkeley Media Studies Group examined how acts of sexual violence are covered by the media. The study found that while the overwhelming majority (91 percent) of coverage was composed of feature stories, they tended to focus on the criminal legal aspects of the case (arrests, trials, and so on) as the "news hook."[8] As the authors of the report wrote, "Child sexual abuse happens every day, but few incidents are covered. . . . Child sexual abuse was most often covered when there was a criminal justice event related to the aftermath, such as an arrest or a trial (73%)."[9] In other words, while child sexual assault cases are underreported, meaning many never come forward to place a formal report, when they are reported, the reporting angle is on a criminal response to the perpetrator of the violence, rather than on the impact and healing experiences of the survivor. Very few films or other entertainment outlets have focused on the experiences of young survivors of sexual violence, which is not surprising given that globally, the exploitation, grooming, and abuse experienced by children in the entertainment industry are routine. A 2024 report by the United Nations found that "predatory sexual behaviour has been accepted as the norm in the entertainment industry because directors, producers, managers and agents have faced no repercussions for unlawfully wielding power and authority over young and vulnerable aspiring entertainers."[10] Perpetrators of violence against children, or anyone who may be complicit in these acts, are not the ones who can responsibly and reliably tell their stories.

"How do you think the public should be expressing care?" I asked Tarana. "How do we invest in girls to interrupt this cycle of violence?"

I have heard girls across the country excuse the behavior that harms them because they've resigned themselves to it. They feel powerless to change it. I remember being in a detention facility where the girls there justified being commercially sexually exploited because prostitution was "the oldest profession in the books."

The girls said to me, "It's always been the way."

"But," I said to Tarana, "there are people like us who actually believe that while the sexual exploitation of women and girls may have always *been,* that doesn't mean it's the way it has to *be.*"

Tarana leaned forward and said, "The *strategy* that I think we have to employ is one of multiple interventions. There is no way that we can shift from what has always been through just policy change or just culture. To move toward what's possible, we need *multiple* interventions. This means that we have to have buy-in on several levels. The most obvious and apparent place for investment for *my* work is in Black women. Black girls grow up to be Black women and Black women carry the care, the connection."

What does it mean that "Black women carry the care"? It means that Black women have to hold onto the personal memories, consciousness, and experiences to bridge understandings. The experiences and lessons of Black girlhood do not disappear upon adulthood. Nor does the awareness of possible interventions to protect girls suddenly appear through osmosis when a young person reaches the age of twenty-one The connections are the iterative healing processes and programs that build communities of care around our girls. These relationships expose them to the value of taking advantage of a host of interventions as the primary way to weave together a quilt of protection. The connection of care is knowing that the health of our girls often determines the health of the community, and the health of the community is reflected in the health of its girls.

"In the #metoo movement, we are thinking about this all the time," Tarana continued. "We are looking at this from multiple angles. You have to start with the people who are most affected. So, investing in Black women is the best way, the *first* way to start. Then you'll get investment into Black girls, because we're going to get our children. And this is important, because there are so many ways that Black girls are in danger. There's not enough medical research on what happens over time to a Black child, a little Black girl who has experienced this kind of trauma. What type of teenager does she become? What type of adult does she become? What are the physical ailments that have developed as a result of her traumas?"

Tarana's questions are important, because they flag the connection between gender-based violence and the ability of girls to grow into healthy adults. The leading causes of death among women are heart disease, cancer, stroke, chronic lower respiratory disease, and Alzheimer's disease.[11] Many of the preventable diseases that affect women are the result of social conditions such as abusive relationships; economic inequality such as unemployment and labor exploitation; environmental factors such as prolonged exposure to toxins released by chemical plants; and other disparities, such as racial discrimination that prevents lifelong access to quality care. But the physical impact of trauma is also associated with poor health outcomes. What is not investigated as much are the ways that trauma impacts communities beyond the physical manifestations of harm. Tarana probed more deeply into the question of how Black women, who were once girls living with the stress of racialized violence, experience risk factors that might render them vulnerable to preventable diseases.

"For instance, what is the prevalence of neurological disorders in the Black community based on these traumas?" she asked. "These are questions that need to be answered. I had a stroke a few years ago, and since I had a stroke, I have run into so many Black women who have either had strokes or various other types of neurological conditions that they've developed over time. We're in our forties! Our fifties! Where does that come from and why is nobody looking at that? There needs to be an investment in research, so that's another intervention: a medical one. We need legal interventions and cultural interventions. I'm all about representation, that's great, but a particular type of representation matters. We need stories that are really about the material lives of Black girls, the nuances, the reality of what it is to live and exist in this country as a Black girl, and what that actually means. So many women have come to me to talk about perfectionism as a result of trauma."

"We don't really talk about that," I interjected.

"And those of us in the community of so-called *Black Excellence* and *Black Achievement*—that's a reaction to something. We've had to overperform and over–show up, which deteriorates our health because we don't know how to rest. We don't know how to stop. Our engine has to keep going. That comes from an unhealed trauma. So now we are having strokes and heart attacks, and nobody's making those connections.

"We're gonna die at the hands of slogans like 'Black Excellence' if we don't take a step back from them and say, *This is not healthy*," she continued. "We've got to tell a different story and talk about what we actually live, not something that was made up and greenlit by Hollywood."

As she was talking, I began to think of the complicated and deeply frustrating nature of the entertainment industry when it comes to stories about the vulnerabilities of girls. The industry is rampant with images that sexualize girls, adultify them, and render them vulnerable to the salacious imaginations of predators. On occasion, a meaningful episode of a television show will discuss these issues, but they are few and far between. In 1981, I remember watching an episode of the sitcom *The Facts of Life*, a TV show I adored, where Natalie (played by Mindy Khan) experiences an attack. In the episode, the physical assault ignites in her a fear of moving forward, and Natalie opts for reading alone and avoids going on outings with her schoolmates. Later, she and the other girls in her dormitory take up self-defense as a strategy to feel empowered when they are in physical danger. Tender from my own history of sexual violence, I understood why Natalie would retreat to reading, burying herself in the comfort of a book. Natalie's fear was palpable, but I also felt a deep affinity with Jo—the show's confident and strong character who regularly defied the gender norms associated with dress, hobbies, and other activities associated with girls at the time. I remember spending time alone after watching the episode and deciding that I could also be a fighter like Jo. Playing sports—skating, volleyball, basketball, martial arts, and other physical activities—helped me rebuild my confidence, and the leadership that accompanied it. In the 1990s, television shows such as the popular sitcom *A Different World,* which explored life on the campus of a fictional Historically Black College, took on gender-based violence on college campuses, across its many forms, addressing intimate partner violence and sexual assault; and in the 2020s, the popular medical drama *Grey's Anatomy* tackled the issue of the particular risk to Black girls of kidnapping and commercial sex trafficking. Such nuanced and intersectional treatments of the topic of gender-based violence were educational, not just entertainment, and as such, they remain anomalous across the industry.[12]

"We spend a lot of time in the world trying to make ourselves whole, because we've been so marginalized from mainstream conversations about wellness, health, and sexual agency," I said. "And we'll always continue to explicitly name Black girls and women in this discussion; but how does this work then extend into the broader world? I think #metoo is probably one of the best examples of a practice that was under way with Black girls, growing to reach a wider audience of survivors."

"I've spent my entire life working in Black communities. My entire life," Tarana responded. "It's a privilege that I have worked with Black women and Black children. It's just what I do. So when #metoo took off, and it was White women and all other women, I didn't know what to say—or what to do. But what was fascinating to me was that it wasn't different. Once that world was opened up to me, I was like, *Oh my God,* y'all, it's the same thing! There was literally nothing different about the messaging. Our mission statement says we are a Black feminist organization rooted in Black Feminist Theory because Black feminism is what got me here and it's all the things that these people love and want and appreciate. If you start with the people who have the least, everybody benefits. Indigenous and Black girls have always been at the bottom rung, so you have to put every effort into making sure that these folks have what they need. It is the fastest and best way for everyone else to get what they need."

I watched Tarana look down at her hands, and then look back up at me.

"I believe so deeply in collective care, and I really believe deeply in community, but that's not to the exclusion of anybody else," she said. "We absolutely need each other. Collective care is the only path forward, and that means that you may have a scratch, but if somebody has a stab wound, you need to deal with the stab wound *collectively*. We've got to take care of the person with the stab wound first."

"You're right!" I jumped in. "If we collectively figure out how to address the stab wound, then the scratch becomes even easier to address. The surface wound becomes easier to address. Yes, I get it."

"The problem is," Tarana continued, "folks with the surface wounds act like they've got stab wounds, which is where education comes in. I've leaned into data, because when you start to explore, you see what a real stab wound looks like. It doesn't mean that your pain does not exist from the scratch, but it does mean that there's a deeper wound that needs to be addressed and that we need to find a remedy for in order for us to quickly and efficiently address all of our needs."

"I love that analogy," I said. "It's powerful."

Just like her.

Legal and executive orders that undermine the right to bodily autonomy for girls and young women are not limited to sexual and other physical acts of gender-based violence. Public narratives that are amplified by biased and repressive digital and broadcast media, as well as policy agendas, also produce conditions that challenge girls' ability to make the final decision about health conditions affecting their bodies.

In the summer between my sophomore and junior years of college, I won an internship with People for the American Way, one of the nation's oldest civil liberties organizations. It was 1992, and at the time, its primary concern was keeping ultraconservative stances on legal access to abortion from prevailing in the Supreme Court's decision on *Planned Parenthood v. Casey.* This case challenged five provisions of the Pennsylvania Abortion Control Act of 1982 that were considered unconstitutional in the debate on whether a person had a legal right to an abortion.[13] I was new to Washington, D.C., at the time, and interested in learning about how politics informed policy. I was interested in learning about how ordinary people could make the federal government see them, respect them, and respond to them.

As an intern, my initial tasks were rudimentary, consisting mainly of updating the mailing list. I was willing to pay my dues and do the grunt work that didn't exercise my growing experience and knowledge as a budding scholar if it meant that I could learn how political advocacy "worked" in D.C. But I also wanted to offer what I could to the organization as it developed its own analysis around a growing crisis having to do with Haitian immigration. I advocated to take the lead on a research project on the subject, which developed into a full report on Haitian immigration and the crisis of the U.S. response. I was proud of that work, and it awarded me some kudos within the organization. One day, my supervisor came into our shared intern office workspace, and announced that in response to the threat of a decision on *Planned Parenthood v. Casey* overturning key elements of *Roe v. Wade,* the landmark case that protected women's reproductive rights, we would be meeting the next day at the steps of the Supreme Court for a demonstration.

The next day, I arrived amid a protest already in motion. People were holding signs and chanting in front of the courthouse. I jumped right in, walking and chatting with other protesters until a man walked out of the building and away from the antiabortion-rights demonstrators. I found myself face-to-face with this man. He could barely look at me, but I stared at him. Immediately, I felt overwhelmed by anger that this man who would *never* carry a child had so much to say about what I might do with my body—and the difficult decisions I might have to make about it. I was incensed that any man would want to control the decisions about the bodies of people who give birth, especially when other forms of gender-based violence are so prevalent. My personal feelings and experiences with reproductive rights aside, I have always believed that any decision about reproductive health should be between a patient and her doctor. Period.

I remember yelling alongside other women in the crowd about a "woman's right to choose." Because I didn't recognize him, I didn't see my communication with him as a personal attack. In that moment, he was every person who wanted to make blanket decisions about the bodies of women and girls, and other birthing people.

He stepped in front of me, and so I said something about how his lack of proximity to the decisions women and girls make about their bodies disqualifies him from that decision. I mentioned how Black women are often subjected to sexual violence and have to make hard decisions about their bodies that he, as a White man, would never know.

I left the demonstration that day, not thinking much of that particular interaction, but grateful that I had the opportunity to participate in something meaningful. Beyond marching and holding signs, I was able to articulate a concern that moved my soul. As a survivor, I was able to name the source of my own sexual trauma, and as a developing scholar, I was able to apply it to policy decisions being made in real time. I felt proud. I felt seen. And I felt tired, so I went back to my apartment and went to sleep.

The next day, as I walked through the office, I noticed people smiling at me.

Then, someone said, "Nice job. Front page, baby!"

I didn't know what that meant, until I got to my shared office and saw that someone had placed a copy of *USA Today* on my desk. On the cover was an image of me with a brown-and-black kufi on my head and cat-eye glasses covering the top portion of my face. My mouth was agape, as I was obviously mid-sentence. My right hand held tightly onto a sign as my left hand pointed a finger in the direction of the man's face. His head was tilted downward, as if he were pensive, and listening to me with care. It was a compelling image—a Black young woman in African attire seemingly shouting into the face of a White man in a Western suit. It certainly appealed to all of the narratives about the vulnerable versus the powerful, but it was not a full reflection of what I was feeling that day or what the fight for reproductive rights was really all about. For the time being, abortion rights were protected. But, as Tarana said about sexual violence, the work to love and protect our girls is about our *collective* wellness. My takeaway from that day and the experience of being on the cover of a national newspaper was that even if the public has been led to believe that they have a say in a person's agonizing decision about their pregnancies—my documented advocacy even led to some tense conversations with elders in my own family—women's rights were worth fighting for. I believed then, and believe now, that women should have the final say in policies that regulate our bodies, and our toughest decisions.

The abortion rights protest was my second major experience with peaceful protest in Washington, D.C. In 1991, as a first-year college student, I went with a group of students to openly protest the Gulf War in Iraq. I was interested in disrupting the severe damage that soldiers had to endure during war, and upon their return. I'd read *Bloods* in high school, a book that captures the oral histories of Black veterans who served in Vietnam.[14] In those stories, I recognized what I'd heard about my uncles' journeys in the military. Like so many other Black men, my uncle Robert had served, only to come back to the United States, where he was forced to endure racial discrimination that resulted in limited opportunity for recovery from war, such as mental health services, treatment for addiction, and finding housing and employment. In addition to its obvious impacts on the physical and psychological well-being of soldiers, war is an appalling form of gender-based violence that impacts the livelihood of girls and young women in many ways. Girls and young women make up a disproportionately high percentage of survivors of soldiers killed or harmed in combat, and they are the majority of people who receive them when they come back to their home communities.

One of my earliest memories involves a morning walk with my mother to the bus stop. We always left our apartment at the same time to ensure that we caught the bus without issue. Usually it was a mundane experience, but that morning, as we approached the bus stop, my mother said, "That's your uncle."

"Where?" I asked. The only person I saw was an unwell man, dressed in ragged clothing and sitting on the sidewalk curb, talking to someone the rest of us could not see.

She walked up to him confidently, holding my brother in her arms. I stood next to her, holding on tightly to my backpack by the straps wrapped around my shoulders.

"Robert," she said. "Do you know who I am?"

He looked at her with confusion and then dismissal. He didn't recognize her, so she let out a sigh and said to me, "Come on," as we walked away.

He continued to focus his attention on whatever he found captivating about the ground and didn't say another word to us. As the bus approached and slowed to allow us to board, my mother walked on first. I saw him look over at us, so I looked away. I'd heard of an uncle with his name, but since he wasn't active in our lives, I felt no emotional attachment to him—and his illness made me uncomfortable at that young age. Then, just as I was stepping onto the bus behind my mother, in my peripheral vision I saw him stand. I hurried onto the bus, fearful that he was going to attack us. But it wasn't anger or rage he was exhibiting, it was excitement.

"Katie!" I heard him yell.

My mother heard it, too, as she settled into her seat near the window. I sat next to her and saw him stand and wave vigorously as the bus pulled away. He smiled, his entire face now beaming with excitement.

"Katie! Hi!" he yelled.

My mother forced a smile and waved back unenthusiastically. I watched her wipe away tears that were starting to stream down her cheeks, but she said nothing. Neither did I. She went to work, and I went to school as if nothing happened. My uncle's experience has impacted how I felt about war since I was a very young person: I've never been an enthusiastic supporter.

As an adult, I have a deepened appreciation for how my mother must have felt, and how connected their health was as siblings. The degree to which our collective health is intertwined makes the consideration of mental health imperative if we are to create systems that fully respond to girls in our society. Even as a girl, I was aware of how challenging it is to manage the unwellness of a loved one. One of my siblings was diagnosed early with severe mental health conditions that would continue to test the stability of our family for many years. It's not easy. And yet I was expected to continue to be a high-performing student and reliable eldest of five children, even as I had no idea how to negotiate mental health issues. I, too, struggled with undiagnosed anxiety and depression for years.

In middle school, while I was trying to reconcile the pain of an absentee father and several other conditions that threatened my well-being, I remember considering the thing that made me recoil as a young reader. Suicidal ideation among young people was not something that people openly discussed in that era, and in school, the most I heard about it was that it was a sin.

"God doesn't forgive the taking of your own life," one of the sisters in my Catholic elementary school warned my class. I heard it clearly, and it settled in my heart.

But one day, I remember staring out the window, wondering what would happen if I jumped. I remember feeling a lot of pressure—being the eldest child is no joke, and I had to take on responsibilities that often felt overwhelming. While my grades were stellar, I was still feeling isolated and unheard. I was still grappling with my own experiences with gender-based violence and thought that everything might be better if I just ended it. I grabbed the window in my bedroom and shook the base to lift it. It rose a little bit, but then stalled. I leaned in to force the window higher, because if I were going to get through it, it needed to be raised more than a few inches. I leaned in so hard that the glass broke and shattered around my arms. My mother came running into my bedroom to ask what happened. Crying, I just told her that the window broke when I was trying to raise it, but I never mentioned why I was trying to get it open. The tiny scars on my wrists and the middle finger of my right hand are barely visible today, but the memory of that day lasts.

Thank God for sports in my life! I discovered basketball and softball in middle school, and later went on to add field hockey to my list in high school. Being on those teams helped me build relationships and provided a mode of physical expression that made me feel powerful and safe. In college, my formal participation in sports was replaced by being active on the step team for my sorority, Delta Sigma Theta Sorority, Inc. Founded on January 13, 1913, on the campus of Howard University, Delta Sigma Theta is a global public-service sorority of primarily Black, college-educated women who elevate sisterhood, scholarship, service, and social action to improve conditions in our communities. In the fall semester of 1991, I pledged Rho Chapter at Columbia University, where I worked hard to embody our public motto, "Intelligence Is the Torch of Wisdom." I led several service projects on my college campus and in the greater Harlem area. I was eventually elected to become my chapter's president, but citywide, I became enamored with stepping—a rhythmic, syncopated dance style rooted in the African and African Diasporic traditions of drumming and circle dancing. With my sorority sisters, I relaunched the New York City Delta Step Team, which had been dormant for a short while, and eventually became a step master—a choreographer of the steps the team performs—and team leader as we performed along the East Coast. These outlets—to practice leadership, express frustrations, and release tensions that might have otherwise led to other outcomes for me and those closest to me—saved my life. Without my sorority, I might never have understood the redemptive and healing power of sisterhood. I might never have formed the bonds with like-minded women who were collectively striving to make meaningful impact on the world. I might never have found the safety of knowing that my mental and physical well-being could be the trusted responsibility of other young women. It prepared me for the next stages of challenging gender-based violence in my life.

These experiences taught me that girls' health is connected to the wellness of everyone in their communities. Acknowledging the reciprocal relationship between the health of the community and the health of our girls is an essential tool for making sound investments in the health sector.

Girls and young women are most at risk of Intimate Partner Violence (IPV), the physical, sexual, or emotional abuse of an intimate partner.[15] Globally, nearly a quarter of adolescent girls aged fifteen to nineteen have experienced physical and/or sexual violence from an intimate partner.[16] According to UNICEF, in 2017, about 15 million girls aged fifteen to nineteen had been forced to have sex in their lifetime, with only 1 percent of these adolescent girls ever seeking professional help.[17] According to the World Health Organization, lifetime intimate partner violence affects 20 percent of women in the Western Pacific, 22 percent of women in high-income countries and Europe, 31 percent of women in the Eastern Mediterranean Region, 33 percent on the African Continent, and 33 percent of women in Southeast Asia.[18] Unfortunately, cases of girls' and women's lifetime experience with intimate partner violence remain grossly underreported, thereby giving the public only a snapshot of the scope of the problem.

Poverty has been proven to increase girls' and women's vulnerability to human trafficking, domestic violence, and loss of income in association with seeking refuge from abusive partners.[19] Girls and young women with disabilities between the ages of sixteen and twenty-five are more likely to live in poverty than those without disabilities, and they experience the lowest levels of educational attainment.[20]

IPV has several mental and physical health consequences as well, including hunger associated with poverty or economic insecurity, physical injury, sexually transmitted diseases, and psychiatric conditions such as depression and post-traumatic stress disorder.[21] Across the United States, 25 percent of girls have self-harmed, which is twice the rate for boys,[22] and the rates of those seriously considering attempting suicide, making a plan for it, and actually trying to do it have all increased for girls.[23] In the U.S., the risk of violent victimization is greater for women and girls than for boys and men, and particularly acute for people who identify as gay, lesbian, bisexual, or trans.[24]

Girls in the U.S. have a higher likelihood of experiencing

Adverse Childhood Experiences (ACEs), or childhood traumas, than their male counterparts,[25] which impacts their ability to be well children and, eventually, to be well adults.[26] While not everyone experiences lifelong impacts of childhood trauma, the stress hormones that develop in response to that trauma produce conditions in the body that increase the risk of heart disease, diabetes, cancer, stroke, obesity, and addiction.[27] Some of these conditions are the leading causes of death among women. Childhood trauma also produces a host of psychological effects, including but not limited to suicidal ideation, anxiety, lack of trust, and low self-esteem.[28] And, while not all girls will eventually give birth, approximately 57 percent between the ages of fifteen and forty-nine do,[29] which can mean that the untreated, unresolved trauma of the mother may transfer to the infant, continuing the cycle of transgenerational trauma.[30] Exposure to childhood trauma disproportionately impacts girls. Girls' exposure to violence and experience with childhood trauma increases as their proximity to poverty increases, but *every* girl is at risk.

Among Native American /Alaska Native people, the average ACE score, the primary tool used to measure childhood trauma, for girls and women is 2.52, which is higher than their male counterparts (2.12).[31] The ACE scores for Indigenous people who identify as gay, lesbian, or bisexual is even higher: gay or lesbian (4.05), bisexual (3.22), as compared with heterosexual (2.21).[32] These scores do not reflect the historical trauma experienced by Indigenous people, nor does it consider some of the specific ways that erasure factors into the ongoing harm of gender-based violence. One of the most egregious examples of the risk of gender-based violence is the rate of missing and murdered Indigenous girls and young women. According to The Red Road, a nonprofit organization that seeks to "empower and minister hope to Native communities" and educate the public about the history and contemporary conditions of Indigenous culture, "the United States and Canada are facing a crisis when it comes to the issue of missing and murdered Indigenous women (MMIW) and girls."[33] While there are no reliable counts of the Indigenous women and girls who are killed or go missing each year, often because their racial identity is misclassified as Latine or only according to other ethnicities and/or racial groups represented in their lineage, their rate of violent victimization (84 percent over their lifetime) far exceeds that of non-Native women. According to the Urban Indian Health Institute, more than 5,700 cases of missing and murdered Indigenous women were reported in 2016, but only 116 were logged into the database of the U.S. Department of Justice.[34]

Black girls, too, go missing at higher rates than other girls. In 2023, the National Crime Information Center reported that the largest share of young people aged 0–17 reported as missing were Black girls.[35] This is one reason that the Chicago-based girls-serving organization A Long Walk Home has committed for years to a day of solidarity with the Missing and Murdered Indigenous Women and Girls campaign on February 13 to commemorate and call attention to the violence our girls are experiencing on our collective watch.[36] Remedy lies in sisterhood and a collective commitment to act against the harms to girls and women from disproportionately impacted communities. When we help them, we help all of us. The social determinants of health such as economic status, housing stability, education, and others include the statistics for girls, so investing in their safety and wellness improves the overall status of health for a community. Girls typically grow up to identify as women, so investing in their physical, emotional, and mental health increases their capacity to contribute to well families and increase productivity. However, girls' health is important not only because it improves conditions for everyone; improving these conditions for girls is important because the girls are inherently *worthy* of such considerations.

How do we shift the public narrative such that our girls are not treated as disposable? Tia Oros Peters, the president of the Seventh Generation Fund for Indigenous Peoples, has some ideas. The fund is a foundation with the express purpose of supporting the self-determination and sovereignty of Native nations. Tia once shared with me in conversation, "At the core, there is the sense of responsibility, not entitlement. It's a spiritual core." Adults need to double down on our responsibilities to our girls including the critical charge of uplifting their well-being. To protect our girls as they pursue abundant futures, we should ask questions that put them and their health at the center in wellness discussions. Early on, girls need to understand that their mental, physical, and emotional health is essential for them to access and realize their well-being in many other facets of their lives. We should also commit to the following practices in order to reposition girls as an essential lever in the movement for health justice.

- **Understand that girls are worthy of positive health outcomes, and should have access to the highest quality of care.** Discourse on public health care should include specific references to girls and pediatric spaces, using an intersectional lens to more effectively respond to the critical interventions needed to move past treatment and on to wellness. Nine percent of women in the U.S. are uninsured, and the increasing number of girls who rely on emergency room resources to respond to conditions better managed by a primary physician is alarming.[37] While the proportion of teen boys visiting emergency rooms for mental health crises declined, girls experienced a 22 percent increase between 2021 and 2022.[38] Health care and medical professionals should explore gender-responsive interventions and considerations at the earliest stages of their medical education and training, such that girls are not an afterthought in the rendering of care.

- **Teach self-regulation modalities, and encourage girls to honor those skills when they face challenges in real time.** Breathing techniques and other modes for self-care and regulation extend the modalities of healing from gender-based violence to yoga practices, long walks, meditation, bath soaks, and other ways that help to reset the nervous system and develop proactive strategies for managing life's most difficult moments.
- **Respond to Adverse Childhood Experiences with care.** Recognize when girls are in danger and respond with care. The movement from trauma to healing in discourses about responses to childhood trauma is largely informed by the principles of collective care. It is also informed by the guidance of practitioners such as Dr. Nadine Burke Harris, a celebrated pediatrician who founded the Center for Youth Wellness and later became California's first state surgeon general. She encourages us to teach survivors of childhood trauma to be aware of how their traumas can trigger risky behaviors such as smoking, physical inactivity, and other damaging behaviors that increase risk of disease.[39] Invest in therapy of different kinds—such as talk, dance, art, drama—and a host of other wellness practices that allow girls to heal from, rather than merely treat or cope with, their traumas.
- **Actively counter the adultification that impacts girls of color, particularly Black girls, whose experiences with trauma often go unrecognized.** The adultification experienced by Black girls and other girls of color is a unique and dangerous trend that impacts the well-being and safety of all. Investing in public education and developing professional training for those who work with

girls, including medical professionals, are essential ways to counter this bias. This includes a narrative shift that focuses on the specific ways that expressions of childhood and adolescence are informed by a host of conditions including racial bias, parentification, linguistic proficiency, and socioeconomic status. Still, we are talking about children. Name girls when we are talking about girls. Name adult women when we are talking about women, and stop conflating the two.

- **Invest in girls' capacity to improve food security.** Gender-based violence can lead to food insecurity. Women and girls are 60 percent of those experiencing food insecurity worldwide.[40] One in five children go to bed hungry every day,[41] and as many as 14 million of those children live in the United States.[42] In the U.S., 24 percent of women-led households report food insecurity, which was exacerbated by gender-based violence, wage disparities, and job insecurity fueled by health crises.[43] When women leave abusive relationships, they often leave with their children, and if the partner was the primary wage earner, it can make finding sustenance a challenge. According to the U.S. Department of Agriculture, food insecurity rates are highest among single mother households (30.4 percent) and women living alone (9.2 percent).[44] Young women and girls with food and water insecurity are more likely to participate in underground economies that render them vulnerable to gender-based violence and contact with the juvenile court or criminal legal system. To encourage their autonomy and to ensure that girls are developing under the best basic conditions, invest in resources, organizations, and strategies that specifically aim to eradicate food and water insecurity among girls and young women.

- **Create spaces for girls to practice healthy boundaries and wellness practices from an early age.** Encourage social media breaks and minimize exposure to content that leads to body dysmorphia—such as airbrushed and altered photos that endorse an unrealistic standard of beauty—and depression. As adults, it is our responsibility to protect girls from predators, even if they are the "creepy" elder or cool cousin we've known all our lives. Honor girls' sense of *knowing* when they feel that they are in danger, rather than telling them that their feelings are not valid. Teaching them about boundaries early in their lives helps them establish them more easily when they enter late adolescence and adulthood.
- **Encourage sisterhood within communities and across walks of life.** Historical legacies of oppression often keep women and girls from forming the relationships with each other that can counter the negative barriers caused by gender-based violence in their lives. Now is the time to build bridges across identities to counter the ways in which opportunities for partnership are invalidated by practices that silo—and therefore render invisible to the public—girls' experiences with gender-based violence.
- **Create spaces for play and sports.** According to researchers at Arizona State University, girls play sports less than boys across age groups—a function of gender stereotypes about who possesses strength and stamina.[45] The Women's Sports Foundation, a philanthropic organization that resources efforts to promote gender equity in sports, reports that Latine girls experienced the greatest decline among girls playing at least one sport, from 62 percent in 2019 and 2020 to about 53 percent in 2021, and Black girls experienced the greatest decline among girls playing at least two sports.[46] Girls who play sports are less likely to

> have an unplanned pregnancy, less likely to suffer from mental health conditions and crises, and are more likely to have good grades and experience body positivity. I am a CEO today, but my earliest leadership experience was on my high school basketball team when I was co-captain. As a young person who was often navigating gender-based violence and other hostile environments, the basketball court was the one place where I could feel safe and engaged. In fact, being on the basketball team was a tool for my safety. It taught me how to read a crowd. It taught me how to read an opponent. It taught me how I could rely on people to show up for me when they were supposed to, when they train and they commit to their practice. It taught me that I could show up for other people when I train and commit to my practice. It taught me that teamwork is about everyone playing their role and about challenging ourselves to be our best. But it was also about identifying and filling gaps. It was about displaying emotional intelligence and problem solving. It was about fairness. It was about a strategy to achieve a fair win. Girls who get in the game learn not to be relegated to the sidelines. They learn to advocate for themselves. They learn to take responsibility for their own actions and drive forward to realize their unlimited potential.

As the world's technology grows to shrink our distance from one another, we can develop relationships that were previously impossible. Today it is possible for us to connect with and uplift girls all over the world. The global sisterhood that we must develop for these girls is necessary and urgent. As the world's political climate becomes increasingly conservative and xenophobic, the specific needs of girls will be pushed further to the margins. In moments like these, we must rely on the wisdom of girls who understand the importance of creating space for possibility when little seems possible.

To create and sustain a global network of girls, it will require adults who make important decisions that impact the lives of girls (policy, practice, and philanthropic) to be in community with each other. This requires sharing information so that there is a collective metric for evaluating potential impact as legislative and other public policies are crafted. It means convening so key narratives are shared across ponds that only artificially disconnect spirits seeking refuge. Girls, like their older counterparts, are facing profound misogyny in many forms, but the path to remedy is *through* this challenge. Our collective messaging about gender-based violence is an essential investment adults must make in—and for—our girls. Staying silent about the murder and rape of Native/Indigenous girls and young women will not make our conversations about gender-based violence more palatable. Staying silent about the number of incarcerated Black and Brown girls and gender-expansive youth in the U.S. will not make our conversations about the juvenile court system more rigorous. Staying silent about the number of girls who express suicidal ideation or experience bullying online will not make our society more emotionally stable. Staying silent about demagogues who threaten the elimination of programs that support girls in crisis will not make us free. Adults must plant and grow seeds that bear fruits of liberation from repressive and prevailing cultures of misogyny. By investing in girls' education and mentorship, as I share in the next chapter, we move closer to preparing them for a life of unlimited promise.

5

INVEST IN GIRLS' EDUCATION AND MENTORSHIP

I truly believe the only way we can create global peace is through not only educating our minds, but our hearts and our souls.

—Malala Yousafzai, education activist

In 2011, I started to write explicitly about the experiences of Black girls in schools. For five years before *Pushout: The Criminalization of Black Girls in Schools* was published, I embarked on a deep exploration of how girls experience violence in their communities and how that impacts how they learn. Two decades prior, I served on the board of two nonprofits—one in New York and one in California—that focused on girls impacted by the criminal legal system; and for many years, I not only advised a national project on girls and gangs but also served on a statewide committee to reduce racial disparities among youth impacted by California's carceral systems. By the time I was writing *Pushout,* I had interviewed hundreds of girls about their experiences in detention facilities across the nation and was frustrated by the conditions that become apparent when accessing one of the nation's most broken systems. The research I conducted at the National Black Women's Justice Institute, the national organization I founded in 2014 to conduct research, elevate, and educate the public about innovative, community-led solutions to address the criminalization of Black women and girls, revealed that Black girls are the only group of girls disproportionately experiencing exclusionary discipline at every educational level.

Despite making up just 15 percent of the female student population nationwide, Black girls are three times more likely than their White peers to be transferred to an alternative school—learning environments that are designed to meet the needs of students who are at risk of academic failure or who face challenges that interfere with their ability to complete their learning in a traditional school—and four times as likely to be expelled from schools.[1] For the 2017–18 academic year, compared to their White peers, Black girls were:

- Five times more likely to experience out-of-school suspensions and three times more likely to experience in-school suspensions;
- Five times more likely to be transferred to an alternative school;
- More than three times more likely to be arrested on campus;
- Three times more likely to be referred to law enforcement;
- Twice as likely to be restrained;
- More than three times more likely to experience corporal punishment; and
- Nearly twice as likely to be placed in seclusion.[2]

For Black girls, the disparities are experienced from kindergarten through high school. Some racial disparities are more pronounced in certain states and educational levels—in Idaho, for example, Black girls are 12.8 times more likely to experience a school-related arrest than their White peers, with most of those incidents taking place at the high school level.[3] Though not as severely as their

Black counterparts, other girls of color—particularly Indigenous girls and multiracial girls—also disproportionately experience exclusionary discipline at various stages along the discipline continuum in schools, particularly among girls who experience suspensions, referrals to law enforcement, and school-related arrests.[4] Girls are more likely than their male counterparts to experience mental health challenges, stress associated with caregiving in the home, substance use, domestic and intimate partner violence, suicidal ideation, online bullying, and sexual violence;[5] but the responses to these conditions in schools remains punitive and out of alignment with the research that shows an increase in victimization and negative life outcomes when young people experience exclusionary discipline and criminalization.[6]

I had grown tired of people telling me that the girls were "fine" because they were graduating at rates that surpassed boys. We needed a new measure of success, so I wrote a book that discussed the policies, practices, conditions, and prevailing consciousness in schools and beyond that rendered Black girls vulnerable to future contact with the juvenile court or criminal legal systems. I wanted everyone to understand that getting through school *despite* what has happened to you should not be the goal for our girls. Successful educational outcomes should be *because* of the investments we make.

The first place I went to talk about the book was at the August Wilson African American Cultural Center in Pittsburgh, Pennsylvania. I was invited to speak about *Pushout* and the ways to counter the criminalization of Black girls by Kathi Elliott, the visionary founder of Gwen's Girls, an organization whose mission is to "empower girls and young women to have productive lives through holistic, gender-specific programs, education, and experiences."[7] I was excited to connect with Kathi and other women who were leading transformative work with girls in the city. Just before I landed, news broke of a massive fight that had taken place at a local high school involving about thirty girls. The headline for a news article on the issue read, "Charges Expected after a 30-Girl Fight at Pittsburgh High School," which could signal only one thing: tongues would be wagging about Black girls in a way that was destined to be unfavorable. Tensions were high—and there I was, someone from out of town, about to talk about why we need to create systems beyond exclusionary discipline.

That night, I tried to be as thorough as possible. More than a lecture, I tried to give a full teach-in on the causes and correlates associated with the conflicts of girls in schools. I gave examples of how policies like zero tolerance undermined the necessary discretionary decision-making power of school leaders who actually knew the children they educated. I shared how practices such as handcuffing seven-year-old girls unfairly criminalized normal adolescent behavior. I explained how the prevailing consciousness about Black girls—what we think about them—was steeped in harmful stereotypes and dangerous tropes about their identities. I covered as much as I could in the two hours I had with that community of educators, youth workers, students, parents, and others, because I understood what was at stake for them—and for all of us. Later that evening, during the Q&A, I sat on stage while the audience took turns probing deeper into what I'd shared. Girls in the audience asked me pointed questions. One by one, they asked questions like, *Why can't people just see what we go through*? Or, *Why can't people see who I am, not what they imagine? Why are adults always worried about what I'm wearing?* They were directed at me, but these questions were really intended for the adults in their community. Finally, the superintendent of schools raised her hand, identified herself, and posed the question I was waiting for all night . . . *What about the fight with thirty girls?*

After responding that it is likely these girls fit the profile of trauma and risk that I'd spent two hours discussing, I invited the superintendent to be in touch with me so that I could support her leadership on this as much as possible. Eventually, she did follow up, and we discussed a strategy for her to connect directly with each of the girls involved in the fight. Some time passed, and then I got a call from her sharing that she'd done just as I suggested, and discovered what we knew all along: girls who don't feel safe, fight.

But that evening brought another revelation. After the lecture and book signing, I went into the restroom to freshen up. As I was washing my hands, a girl quietly walked up to me and said, "You say what I feel."

I paused and thanked her for telling me that. She looked down at the floor—or my shoes—and nodded, and then walked out of the bathroom with me. When she said that, I realized that my work to advance educational equity was not only important, it was *essential.* I was very clear that from that point forward, no matter the crowd size, no matter where I was in the world, girls were trusting me to *say* what they *felt.* And that was not an assignment I took lightly. I went on a book tour—but it wasn't your average tour. I spoke at school board conferences, teacher convenings, and at individual schools. I spoke to students across the educational spectrum. I spoke to police officers and judges. I spoke to medical professionals. I spoke to social workers. I spoke to the U.S. Civil Rights Commission. I spoke to federal and state legislators. I spoke to philanthropists. The more I went out in community, the more evident it became that the women leading girls-serving organizations experienced many of the same conditions as the girls who attend their programs or who were impacted by their advocacy and/or research. Because of their shared experiences, I realized that they were walking the learning and advocacy journeys *together* to fight against the tropes and stereotypes that we assign to "girlhood," and Black girlhood in particular.

The gift of writing *Pushout* is that it became so much more than a book. Ultimately, it has become a project that gives us the freedom to explore how to have *all* girls' best interests at heart in educational settings. It has allowed us to consider how schools may actualize my call to engage our girls as sacred and loved. I followed *Pushout* with *Sing a Rhythm, Dance a Blues: Education for the Liberation of Black and Brown Girls,* which provided a framework for responding to school pushout by centering on this Appreciative Inquiry: *How do schools become locations for healing so that they realize their potential as locations for learning?* I offer a specific framework for activating this inquiry—to move past "reform" to a more intentional embrace of "restructuring our entire approach to the education of Black and Brown girls in crisis."[8] I know that if adults who work with girls structure their policies, activities, and other interventions to ensure they reach the girls who are most historically marginalized, we will finally be able to invest in and respond to the needs of *all* girls. I described several remedies being taken by schools and other learning environments across the country and offered examples of educators countering pushout by employing devices rooted in trauma-responsive strategies for girls, including restorative approaches, advocacy, art, and affinity group discussions, among others.[9]

Pushout and *Sing a Rhythm, Dance a Blues* were the basis for my documentary film *Pushout,* where Women in the Room Productions—a small production company based in Los Angeles owned by media and business pioneers Denise Pines and Jacoba Atlas—and I brought to life some of the narratives about adultification and criminalization in schools. As the co-writer and one of the executive producers of the film, it was my goal to reach as many people as possible with the message that our schools do not have to usher in a generation of learners with violence and rejection when they are dysregulated. Emotional dysregulation, the inability to control one's emotions and the expression of these feelings, and dissociation are responses to trauma.[10] Girls sometimes make mistakes, and when they do, we should respond to them with best practice, not bias. Trauma specialist and author Bessel van der Kolk attests that, "As long as trauma is not resolved, the stress hormones that the body secretes to protect itself keep circulating, and the defensive moments and emotional responses keep getting replayed . . . if elements of the trauma are replayed again and again, the accompanying stress hormones engrave these memories ever more deeply in the mind."[11] For this reason, I have been campaigning for schools to be locations for healing. For too many girls, the trauma of arrest and other forms of emotional, physical, and sexual violence take place at school, thereby transforming school into a hostile environment. Healing from these experiences requires that educators, advocates, and students work together to foster spaces for girls that shift how they tackle the hardest part of shaping our responses to girls. What we think about them, and how our thoughts lead to actions that either support their well-being (for example, through counseling and relationship building), or deepen the harm (relying on suspensions, expulsions, or other forms of exclusionary discipline) is a critical, yet undertheorized, part of our work to ensure that our girls are not limited by the biases and fears of adults.

Ultimately, the film *Pushout* aired on PBS, placed and won awards at several festivals across North America, and was viewed in communities across the country via private screenings and at local and federal government agencies. It was nominated for an NAACP Image Award in 2020. But the true gift of the film was that it sparked action in communities. Education, like justice, is a local project. Schools, indeed, individual classrooms, engage in practices that impact the learning outcomes and educational attainment of our young people. Different communities have different educational systems, infrastructures, and practices. This meant that if I wanted to influence the educational outcomes of our girls, and not just write about theory and trend data, I would have to go into those communities to talk to people on the ground.

I found that students across the gender continuum often liken their schools to carceral institutions, so the work that I began with Black girls now reaches many more young people in our schools who are targeted for exclusionary discipline.

"My school feels like a prison," many students have shared with me.

"What do you want your school to feel like?" I would typically ask.

"Safe . . . like a sanctuary," one girl from Louisiana once said.

What we do to facilitate the safety of a sanctuary is very different from what we do to facilitate a prison. The kinds of structures we build, the expectations we have, the people we bring in, the way that we invite people to be in community with each other—all these are different if we are building a sanctuary, versus a prison.

Educators, parents, and advocates must invest in girls' education by creating learning environments that are healing centered and trauma-responsive for every student. Becoming trauma-responsive, therefore, is a first step, a foundational part of investing in the well-being of girls. Philadelphia clinician Dr. Sandra Bloom introduced the concept of the Sanctuary Model in the early 1980s as a "blueprint for clinical and organizational change."[12] This healing-centered praxis includes 1) *trauma theory,* the understanding that "many of the behavioral symptoms that we see in individuals are a direct result of coping with adverse experiences"; 2) *parallel processes,* the recognition of the interconnectedness between individuals and institutions requiring a two-pronged approach that addresses both; and the *Seven Sanctuary Commitments,* which are a commitment to nonviolence, a commitment to emotional intelligence, a commitment to inquiry and social learning, a commitment to democracy, a commitment to open communication, a commitment to social responsibility, and a commitment to growth and change.[13] Since 2018, Gwen's

Girls in Pittsburgh has employed this Sanctuary Model in its interactions with girls to "promote safety and recovery from adversity through the active creation of a trauma-informed community."[14] Using the Sanctuary Model as a "restorative approach to help girls heal from trauma," Gwen's Girls has convened community meetings with girls before the start of program work and at check-ins, and its seven commitments have been incorporated into the performance review and supervision activities of administrators.[15] This framework exemplifies what I mean when I say that our institutions should receive our girls as sacred and loved. It's sacred inquiry in action.

For years, people have conflated the educational attainment of girls with their actual well-being in learning spaces. Far too many times, I'd hear, "The girls are fine. They're graduating, so they must be fine!" But I've always been clear that there's more to the story. While on paper, girls appear to be doing quite well, they are moving in educational spaces often *despite* what is happening in their lives, not *because of* the investments we are making in their lives and well-being. That simple shift provides an opportunity to then ask, What do we need to have in place to facilitate wellness, and not just prove how resilient girls are? Resilience is the power to recover in the face of adversity. But our collective goal should be to make their educational journey less adverse in the first place.

To ensure that schools are places that facilitate girls' well-being, the investments we need to make include building a robust continuum of alternatives to exclusionary discipline and implementing curricula that strengthen students' critical thinking skills across academic disciplines. Strategies for supporting learning and the well-being of girls in schools that respond to trauma and dysregulation with love and research-based interventions include asking questions like "What happened?" and offering to lead young people through breathing exercises that can reduce anxiety. These strategies should take the place of responding to them with fear and law enforcement.[16] Many of these interventions that I and others have recommended over the years are reflected in the federal legislation introduced by Rep. Ayanna Pressley (D-MA), which I co-named the Ending Punitive, Unfair, School-based Harm that Is Overt and Unresponsive to Trauma Act of 2023, or the Ending PUSHOUT Act. Originally introduced in 2019 and reintroduced in 2023, the bill calls for three primary actions: 1.) it requires the Department of Education to award grants to local educational agencies and nonprofit organizations to reduce the overreliance on exclusionary discipline; 2.) it requires the Department of Education to collect and monitor data on exclusionary discipline in schools; and 3.) it establishes a joint task force to end school pushout.[17] These practices are foundational for ensuring equal access to a quality education, as they create an infrastructure to respond to the root causes of the disparities, and are not just symbolic gestures or representational quotas. The act was accompanied by a request for the Government Accountability Office (GAO) to conduct an independent review of the conditions in schools to determine if there is, indeed, differential treatment of Black girls in schools. In 2024, the results of that study were released.

As I have documented since 2011, the GAO report confirmed that Black girls do, in fact, face harsher treatment in schools. In a report titled *Nationally, Black Girls Receive More Frequent and More Severe Discipline in School than Other Girls,* the GAO documented with granularity the way that racial biases inform the decisions made on subjective infractions such as defiance, disrespect, noncompliance, and on objective infractions such as property damage or technology violations, etc., in schools. The report found that the factors associated with increased discipline for girls include eligibility for free or reduced-price lunch, which is a proxy for students living in poverty; whether girls are living with disabilities; whether a teacher is new; the presence of any school resource officer or law enforcement officer working in the school; being in grades 6–12; and being in grades 6–12 with a full-time counselor.[18] The report also discussed the impact of colorism on the disciplinary decisions made in schools—finding that girls with darker skin tones were more likely to be suspended than those with lighter skin tones.[19]

In late 2024, to announce the findings of the GAO report, Rep. Pressley held a press conference on Capitol Hill and invited me to speak. I walked through the building's large wooden doors and down a long hallway, eventually arriving at the location where cameras were being set up. Staffers were busy setting up chairs, removing tables, and mounting posters that read "Schools are for learning not criminalization," "Let Black girls learn," and "Black girls deserve educational equity." Mounted on the front of the podium was a large sign that read, "Uplift Black Girls: End Pushout."

Rep. Pressley has long been a champion for girls and a partner in my own efforts to generate a policy response to the pushout phenomenon. Known to share that "policy is [her] love language," this bill is one of several that either are centered on the well-being of girls or consider girls as the primary beneficiaries if implemented. In fact, Rep. Pressley—alongside Rep. Dr. Robin Kelly (D-IL) and Rep. Bonnie Watson Coleman (D-NJ)—introduced many federal bills explicitly centered on girls and using an intersectional lens, which recognizes the multiple identities that inform how girls and other young people experience institutions and policies. Rep. Pressley once shared on social media, "I mean bold, robust investments in healthcare, housing, education, climate and transit justice, closing the wealth gap, and more. All of our communities having support and resources they need to thrive? Yes. That's love."[20]

As we waited for the presser to begin, I casually chatted with Rep. Kelly about the core contributors to pushout. As a co-convenor of the Congressional Caucus on Black Women and

Girls, Rep. Kelly has also been an unapologetic advocate for girls in Congress, especially on the issue of health care. We were joined by other partners and advocates on the issue, including Fatima Goss Graves, CEO of the National Women's Law Center, and Dr. Adjoa Asomoah, an architect of the CROWN Act.[21] I have known both women for years, and partnered with them each in different ways to advocate for the well-being of our girls—from brainstorming research to document the racial disparities among girls experiencing school discipline to informally exploring the expansion of scholarship to encourage approaches that better respond to the needs of girls. Also present was Rebecca Amadi from GLSEN, a national network of educators and students working to ensure the safety of LBGTQ+ students in schools. Together, we were ruminating about various aspects of policy that negatively impact women and girls, or that threatened to do so. Then, all of a sudden, the murmurs stopped and the room went quiet.

"Wow . . . a hush really fell over the room," I said to Fatima.

She smiled. "Nancy Pelosi just walked in."

There's a protocol to the political engagements of Washington, D.C. Since Speaker Emerita Nancy Pelosi is one of the most powerful women in federal politics, everyone in the room knew to default to a respectful silence when she entered.

"Shall we go say hi to the Speaker Emerita?" Fatima asked, a knowing smile covering her face.

"Let's go," I said.

We walked over and reintroduced ourselves to her. As her former constituent, I had met her decades earlier in her San Francisco office. I believe I was meeting with her about juvenile justice issues, as that was my primary focus at the time. I remember her eager look, leaning in wherever she found interest when I spoke. I, along with other advocates, were sure to find compelling ways to communicate what we believed to provide promise for the well-being of our Bay Area communities. But this time, years later and in the nation's capital, I was there with her because of an agenda I helped to launch.

Then Rep. Pressley tapped me on my shoulder, and I extended my arms to greet her with a hug. As we embraced, I offered my immediate gratitude to her for leveraging her position to continue to center girls. As the morning progressed, Rep. Rosa DeLauro (D-CT), ranking member of the House Appropriations Committee; Rep. Bonnie Watson Coleman; and Rep. Ilhan Omar (D-MN) all joined the lineup. We marched through the primary findings of the GAO report and why the Ending PUSHOUT Act was an important remedy to the negative educational outcomes for Black girls, and girls of all racial groups.[22] One by one, we elevated the importance of making sure all girls are treated safely, and fairly, in schools.

"We are here to shine a light on the pushout crisis," said Rep. Pressley. "This is a crisis of systemic criminalization and adultification that has caused Black and Brown girls to be disproportionately pushed out of our schools at alarming rates . . . when we discipline and detain our girls, we fail to see their humanity and we fail to see their brilliance."

"The challenge is so unfair to Black girls in America. We have to make this a priority to take up the bill," said Rep. Pelosi.

"Children, children, children . . . these are all of our children," said Rep. DeLauro. "It is further evidence for what we have known for some time . . . this is so damaging to their safety, wellness, and their academic success . . . education has always been the root to success in this nation. Kids are only going to learn if they are allowed to participate in schools and to reach their full potential. We cannot have an education system that tolerates disciplining one group of students differently and more severely than another."

"I have personally supported the Ending PUSHOUT act since 2019 when it was first introduced, and I continue to professionally endorse it as it aligns with many of the research-based best practices associated with creating schools that counter bias and instead, provide a foundation for our young people to be in right relationship with their teachers, their peers, and themselves," I said. "When schools are part of the tapestry of healing in the lives of our children, they feel safe enough to learn and they grow to become well-adjusted adults who walk in their purpose and live with integrity."

"They're losing learning time and bonding time," Fatima said. "And carrying the weight of other people's racial and gender stereotypes."

The morning was exciting and moving, so much so that Rep. Pressley began to cry. "I won't apologize for getting emotional," she said.

Watching her cry, as I stood nearby, I was aware that her tears represented both longing and celebration. The other congresswomen gathered around her and laid their hands on her back and shoulders to signal their support. I intentionally stood back and let them express their support for her as her colleagues and as a collective of policymakers. I knew they would, as women, have to champion that effort together in a Congress that was only 29 percent women, and which often struggled to advance policies that positively and intentionally protected the economic, educational, and physical health of women and girls.[23]

It matters that women hold political office. It matters that we advocate and build relationships with other women who have a close proximity to the issues impacting our communities. Without the interventions and active engagement of people who work with girls, public policy reflects only a narrow perspective about how girls in our communities thrive. One of the reasons the Ending PUSHOUT Act holds so much promise is that it is informed by activists, researchers, and girls (across both of those categories) who have lived through school pushout. Adults who work with, and on behalf of, girls envision a world in which all girls have the opportunity to participate in learning that supports their well-being and responds to their needs. We invest in girls by talking to them and gathering their input—as they are experts when it comes to their own lived experiences. More than the subject of our inquiry, they are the producers of knowledge regarding how we achieve educational equity. Investing in girls' educational equity is scholarly work. It's legislative work. It's friendship work. It's movement work. It's a love work. It's a mentorship work. All of it is *the* work.

Over the years, many women and men have mentored me. These people shared their expertise and guidance in a way that not only shaped my professional career but inspired me to think about my unique gifts and how those might amplify my interests. As a young person, some mentors were older students. As I aged, those people became supervisors or colleagues in my workplaces. I settled into several mentee/mentor relationships with teachers, professors, or other educators because those adults recognized something in me and extended themselves as resources for my development. This has been the model that I have sought to pay forward.

In the mid-1990s, I was working at a public school–affiliated volunteer program in San Francisco when I was tapped to co-chair a committee that was part of a citywide initiative to explore racial disparities in educational outcomes for African American students under the leadership of Superintendent Raul Rojas. My work on that committee gave me a chance to reconnect with organizations doing educational work in the city. In this new position, I was able to visit classrooms, meet with students and teachers, and visit after-school programs affiliated with I.R.I.S.E., the culturally responsive math and language-literacy curriculum being used in the district at that time. Being in this position also afforded me the chance to work closely with other community leaders such as Aileen C. Hernandez, the union organizer, civil rights activist, and women's rights activist who co-founded and served as president of the National Organization for Women between 1970 and 1971. My time with her was particularly rewarding, as we often made visits to schools and organizations together, representing an intergenerational commitment of community support for the education of our children. During one of our visits, she handed me a copy of a book to which she contributed. The 1997 book *Black Women Stirring the Waters* was a collection of essays from prominent Black women advocates for freedom. The jacket cover was black-and-white, with a prominent image of a Black woman moving forward, head tilted toward the sky, presumably on her journey toward freedom. The image was the logo for a group of professional Black women who assembled to discuss "issues and concerns of Black people" and to pool resources to support access to higher education for young African American women and girls.[24] When she handed me the book, I was in the throes of learning how to manage my life as a young, full-time professional. Determined to maintain a healthy work-life balance, I placed the book on my coffee table and went for a run around Lake Merritt in Oakland. I would let it sit there for weeks before opening it to discover the Bay Area's untold stories of Black feminist leadership. Her chapter, titled "Racism and Sexism Must Be Vanquished," caught my attention. It described her childhood journey of navigating society's expectations of girls in the 1930s and 1940s, and her experiences as an emergent scholar at Howard University in Washington, D.C., where she was the only female student in her political science courses. Her experiences underscored the importance of leading through an intersectional lens.

She wrote, "I learned quickly that it was possible for someone to be deeply committed to ending racism (as my professor was) and still be a sexist. Years later, when I was president of the

National Organization for Women (NOW), I understood that it was equally possible for a dedicated feminist, fighting for women's rights, to be a racist. As a black woman, I had no choice except to be involved in both struggles."[25] She encouraged me to write, and to write from my unique perspective. As a result, I published several opinion pieces in the *San Francisco Chronicle* and the local African American paper the *Bay View*. "Our goal must be freedom for all people—male and female—unhampered by irrelevant restrictions based on demeaning stereotypes," she concluded. "It is our only hope for bringing about that long promised humane and equitable society."[26] With her guidance, I left that campaign a stronger, more insightful writer, and a savvy advocate in the field of education.

When that campaign ended, I won a scholarship to participate in a professional development program focused on cultivating San Francisco's next generation of leaders. There I connected with several people who were business leaders growing to advance critical aspects of San Francisco's economy. At the time, I was relatively new to the professional world of the city. Even though I was born and raised in San Francisco, I had a different understanding of what the city, and its leadership, represented. This program connected me with people who would eventually become the chief of police, executives in communications, restaurateurs, and other corporate and finance leaders in San Francisco and beyond. I was still just in my early twenties and had been educated in New York, so I was also building a professional network from scratch. The Black women in the program took a special interest in me, which I appreciated. In them I saw safe spaces and familiar culture. I had been doing my part, and they saw where they could help. In school, I learned the "what" and "how." Through mentorship, I learned the "when" and "who."

I imagine they saw younger versions of themselves in me and wanted to invest their time and energy in my ability to advance.

They complimented me on being polished and articulate and put me in positions that provided me access to opportunities for my skills to flourish. Through them and their willingness to share their networks, I was able to speak about my work on television. I was able to grow my own connections within and across industries in ways that helped me amplify my local profile and positioned me for greater opportunities. I called them my "community mothers," rather than mentors, because the love felt genuine. It was not transactional—mentorship should not be. For that reason, though I have taught and coached many over the span of my life, I have closely mentored only a few girls and young women. I believe that for young women to advance, mentorship must be intentional.

Women and girls make up more than two-thirds of the world's 796 million people classified as "illiterate."[27] The United States has made great strides toward educating women and girls, and we profess to understand its lasting importance. The U.S. Department of State writes, "The benefits [of education] to girls and their families are well-documented, from better health and nutrition for themselves and their children, to delayed marriage and enhanced employment opportunities. Studies show a single year of primary education correlates with a 10–20 percent increase in women's wages later in life; a single year of secondary education results in a 15–25 percent increase. Education is the best tool we have available to reliably change entrenched attitudes and is an important step in breaking the cycle of poverty."[28] This is applied well in global discourses about access to education; however, what I have learned from this fight to end pushout in the U.S. is that many of our girls are still grappling with age-old stereotypes that prevent them from the full realization of their abilities domestically as well. Once people realize the importance of creating schools that are healing-centered and responsive to trauma, we will get closer to the goal of making education accessible to every child. Underlying the vast majority of girls' issues in schools is their risk of, and experiences with, trauma. Measuring our success simply by the number of girls and young women graduating from schools is not enough.

At 16 percent, girls and women are more likely to live in poverty than their male counterparts (13 percent).[29] Young women are underrepresented in nearly every sector of employment among growth industries except health care—and even then, they are underrepresented in senior leadership. Women hold 76 percent of all health care jobs, and more than 85 percent of those are in nursing, psychiatric care, and home health aides.[30] Women represent only 41 percent of physicians and surgeons, which is an access issue—and the access becomes more difficult to reach the farther they are from proximity to men in power. Education is an essential tool of upward mobility, as mentorship is, but more than 60 percent of young women have never had a mentor.[31] Girls and young women under the age of twenty-five experience systemic exclusion from some of the nation's most powerful decision-making structures. They're underrepresented in the sciences and other fields in STEM (science, technology, engineering, and math) because they are tracked away from study in these areas from a very young age. According to the Massachusetts Institute of Technology, the factors that steer girls from STEM areas of study include stereotypes that associate STEM fields with "masculine qualities"; the lack of role models in these fields; unconscious biases in hiring, promotions, and grant funding; and demands of the field that prevent a desirable work-life balance.[32] From medicine to technology and climate change, women and girls across racial groups are managing conditions in and outside of their homes to cultivate the well-being of themselves and their families. Their underrepresentation in STEM fields represents an underrepresentation of analysis, of diversity of thought, of opportunity for the development of truly innovative and transformative strategies to ensure a just and sustainable society. As a result of the COVID-19 global pandemic, the expected timeline for closing the "gender gap has increased by a generation from 99.5 years to 135.6 years."[33] The economic consequences of the pandemic for girls and women are real—impacting their upward mobility, financial security and independence, and quality of life more broadly.

Women are also underrepresented in finance and among many sectors of public leadership, which can design structural and policy responses to this problem. For example, in 2025, women were just 29 percent of congressional representatives and 25 percent of senators.[34] Only 30 percent of statewide elective executive officers are led or co-led by women. Women hold only 31 percent of seats in state legislatures and only 25 percent of our nation's cities are represented by women.[35] All of these are just numbers until you consider that state and federal laws governing economic, educational, reproductive, and other critical decisions that impact women and girls' bodies and living conditions are largely in the hands of legislators who do not identify as female and have never lived life as a girl. Experiential knowing matters. So, too, does mentoring into the leadership of these sectors.

One of my invitations when I talk publicly about efforts to create healthy learning environments for girls is, *Are you going to be part of the tapestry of healing, or the tapestry of harm?* Most of the schools think of themselves as inherently part of the tapestry of healing, but that's not the case. If a school is facilitating harm by activating tools that oppress our students—girls, boys, and gender-expansive youth—then it is functioning to enact harm. If there is someone in a school who doesn't believe in the promise of all children, that person should leave. The only people who should be charged to work with students are those who embrace the idea that no child is disposable. While I believe that most educators go into this work believing in the promise of children and come in with a desire and passion for connecting with young people, they often get administratively worked out of this passion by the demands of paperwork such as record keeping, manual classroom preparation, and other responsibilities.

However, if a school is not a loving place, it can't be a healing place, and thus it cannot be a learning space. For schools to be locations for healing and learning with girls, we must first commit to develop structures centered on their well-being. Who creates infrastructure? People do! Just as we collect data on the issues that are important to us, we create an infrastructure to support our values. We invest in girls' education by cultivating learning spaces that respond to trauma with care and healing opportunities. Educators should encourage girls to express intuitively and with the tools that engage their full sense of *knowing*. All schools should have a robust continuum of responses to dysregulation that includes school-based restorative practices, counseling, and mindful work. The package of life-skills interventions known as SEL (Social Emotional Learning) includes self-awareness, self-management, social awareness, relationship skills, and responsible decision-making skills.[36] Schools should integrate gender-responsive iterations of research-based best practices in SEL. But it's not enough for schools to offer these interventions if they fail to ensure that girls have access to them. Or if the interventions are not implemented in a manner that explicitly considers the components of effective programs for girls. For example, efforts to invest in girls' educational equity cannot only include school-based restorative justice circles. They have to recognize other modalities for restoring relationships, including mentoring, sports, braiding, food care and preparation, visual art, literature, and dance, among others. Girls also need at least one adult on campus that they can rely on as a "safe person." The functionality of this person is part of the healing-centered, trauma-responsive social infrastructure of a school, even if their official position is that of teacher, coach, counselor, or principal.

Other ways to invest in girls' education include:

- Making space for every "type" of girl. Celebrate the nerds, the socialites, the athletes, the emo girls, the Barbies, the dolls, the cis, trans, and gender-fluid girls who express in all ways across the gender spectrum, and more. Showing a girl that she is welcome to bring her *full* self to her learning space allows her to feel as if she belongs in school, which then facilitates the condition where she feels safe enough to learn.
- Ensuring that mentorship and leadership opportunities are available to girls in school. Girls are not always engaged as leaders at school, but they should be encouraged to step forward as such. This strengthens her connection with educators, peers, and the institution itself such that genuine trust, learning, and safe engagement can occur.
- Facilitating spaces where girls can enter areas of academic study in which they have been historically underrepresented. Advocate for and create pathways for girls to study in STEM and other fields where women experience underrepresentation. Girls need intentional/facilitated access to these fields. Where sexism is entrenched, it is difficult for a girl to see her worth. Having access to education and mentors in these spaces is essential.

Many innovative school-based and extracurricular programs exist to amplify the promise of students by connecting them with professionals in their field of interest or by exposing them to communities through travel—and study-abroad opportunities. The problem is that too many of them were not created with girls in mind, or they were created to respond to male students in a way that is perceived as gender neutral. For example, school districts and other youth-serving organizations implemented programmatic interventions to improve student outcomes under My Brother's Keeper (MBK), a broad partnership between government and philanthropy launched by the administration of President Barack Obama in 2014, now a signature initiative of the Obama Foundation. Two years after the initiative's launch, nearly 250 MBK Model Communities existed, with more than $600 million committed in private sector and philanthropic resources, as well as $1 billion in low-interest financing committed in alignment with MBK.[37] Many of the programs in alignment with MBK, which included mentoring, access to jobs and internships, and the reformation of school discipline policies, among others, also served girls. Girls may have taken advantage of the programming that was put in place, but, as I chronicle in *Pushout,* without the explicit focus on girls' experiences, opportunities to address the issues that uniquely impact them (e.g., racialized gender-based violence, etc.) remained unaddressed.

In general, it is a mistake to consider a program appropriate for girls just because girls participate in it. We must also be mindful not to create programs without consideration for the specific needs of girls and then add pink to the color scheme or marketing materials and assume that this gesture will suffice. Amplifying the learning community for girls requires mentorship. A 2023 study conducted in partnership by Être, a mentorship program that connects girls to women leaders, and YPulse, a research-based authority on Generation Z and Millennials, found that 86 percent of girls want a mentor, and that these numbers increase in fields like finance (93 percent) and STEM (86 percent), where there is extreme underrepresentation of women.[38] Être's founder, Illana Raina, said of the study, "Mentors matter because they bolster girls' confidence exactly when they need it most."[39]

Mentorship must include:

- Consistency
- Opportunities to shadow and learn
- Connections and sharing of networks
- Transfer of relationships and opportunities to practice and demonstrate their growth and expertise
- Critical feedback as she grows and explores different opportunities in life. Mentorship is not always about encouragement. Sometimes it's about redirection. Helping a girl lean into her purpose and walk in alignment with her assignment—in life and in school—means that trust has to be established and nurtured.

Over the years, I have aimed to practice this type of mentorship, and to extend my praxis of girls' and young women's development. Two of the young women I have mentored served as core partners in my work. Aishatu Yusuf, like me, was often the only young Black woman leading juvenile justice research in the Bay Area. She reached out to me through a mutual friend in 2012 and we met for breakfast one day near Lake Merritt. Immediately, I was impressed by her intelligence and her willingness to partner with me as a learner, not just as a receiver of information. Our exchange was exciting and I was interested in helping to create spaces for her to shine more brightly. Being a mentor is one of the most important duties of my life. As a mentor, I am signing up to become a person who can guide, inspire, and protect her. But my experiences with mentorship have been rewarding in other ways as well. She helped me build the work and community of the National

Black Women's Justice Institute, which remains the only organization of its kind—a Black women–led think tank on justice and community-led solutions to address the criminalization of Black women and girls.[40]

Years later, in 2020, Maheen Kaleem became another of my mentees. She is the vice president for G4GC, but I first met her as a young advocate working as the only first responder for young people surviving commercial sexual exploitation in the Bay Area's Alameda County. I was always struck by her intellect and curiosity, and by the way that she naturally connected with girls in crisis. One of my earliest memories of her was watching her respond to a girl who was experiencing dysregulation after being triggered by an abusive boyfriend. Maheen's care and kindness were her most compelling qualities, and I could immediately sense the power of her leadership style. When the time came for me to enter the field of philanthropy and build out G4GC as an organization, she was at the top of my list.

"You have allowed me to be in space with you . . . and I find that it's not just mentorship, but love," Aishatu said, when I asked her to reflect on my mentorship. "The beauty of having you as a mentor is when you allow people in—if they choose to soak it all up, they can learn so much about themselves, about work, about life, and about how to be a woman—about how to be a Black woman, how to engage in this world where there's drama, and love, and all of these things. You allowed me to do that, and that's contributed to who I am and who I will become."

Transformative mentoring requires mentoring with your whole self—to share aspects of your life, as an adult and/or seasoned professional, that demonstrate not only what it looks like to do the work, but what it looks like to be a leader in your sphere of influence. For me, that has been essential.

"You gave me the opportunity to decide what I want to learn, and how I want to learn it. I am the person who wants to learn everything all the time, all at once. So, I grabbed *every* opportunity that you gave me. I grabbed every opportunity you gave me as a time to learn and to deepen myself and grow."

My mentor/mentee relationships with these two women is special because they confirm, time and again, that when we provide opportunities for girls and young women to lead, they often seize the opportunity and grow it. I consider them thought-partners in my work with and for girls.

"The first way that you have mentored me is by seeing things in me that I didn't know were there," Maheen said. "But I trusted and respected you enough that even when I couldn't see it, I believed you when you saw it. I think there is a way that you held me accountable to a higher standard, where you said, 'I see you as a researcher. I see you as an advocate. I see you as a legal mind.'"

Being a mentor requires paying attention. Girls and young women are not necessarily looking to be replicas of their mentors. They are looking for guidance to step fully into their purpose.

"What is uniquely yours, and your philosophy about mentorship, is that mentorship is about visibility and love. What you have given me is that you see me. I think mentorship is seeing, particularly for me, seeing people who would not be seen by other people. The other thing I think about mentorship is that you lead with a lot of gravitas and directness, but you tell the people that you are mentoring that you love them. You actually say, 'I love you,' and you lead with love in ways that allow for the traditional notions of mentorship, where you're supposed to have boundaries (which never worked for me). You have always been a human first, and I think it's given me validation around how I mentor."

Aishatu's and Maheen's reflections about mentorship invite me to consider why I was so moved when that girl in Pennsylvania told me, "You say what I feel." Our young people are watching us. Girls need models in their lives to show them what is possible, and to provide opportunities for them to engage their wisdom. My mentorship style leans heavily into role modeling. Beyond representation, helping mentees understand how to live as whole people—frailties and all—gives them tools to navigate life's most pressing challenges. It's important not to present just the pretty picture. Being vulnerable as a mentor to girls and young women is also important. Women and girls are underrepresented in leadership across sectors and institutions, and that means there can often be a perception that there is little room for error. But people do make mistakes. For girls and young women, it's critically important to demonstrate how to manage walking their journey while holding someone else's hand to bring them along. Our success and well-being is not a solo project—it's a collective one. My own practice of mentorship centers on holding girls and young women, whether they are in doubt about their capabilities, or if they are assured and confident. It is about teaching them that doubt is not a deal-breaker, and confidence needs access. A girl can know, a girl can be educated, a girl can be well and healthy—but if she lacks access, she will not be able to apply these skills and qualities in the practice of her leadership. Mentors teach and mentors learn in a lifelong practice; and together, we advance. The work between mentors and mentees is generative, not extractive, and therein lies the unlimited possibility for healing.

6

MAKE THE FINANCIAL INVESTMENT

We have to bring in the capital, we have to organize, we must fight intelligently.

—Mary McLeod Bethune, educator, philanthropist, and civil rights activist

Much of this book explores the nonfinancial investments adults must make in girls—and why they're so important. But let's be real. These investments materialize much faster when they are backed by financial resources. Money matters.

In 2020, I became the inaugural CEO of G4GC. I was excited to lead such essential efforts. For more than a decade prior, I had been raising questions about philanthropic strategies to invest in the well-being of girls, particularly girls of color. I wanted to know why foundations that supported girls were not explicit in their language and mission about wanting to resource organizations that also have a strong racial analysis. I wanted to know how to make the well-being of all girls a priority across large philanthropic efforts. I wanted to know how to end girls' erasure in big philanthropic efforts. I wanted to know why the giving was so scarce in the first place, and what we could do to change that. As if to further deepen this inquiry, just as I was entering the world of philanthropy to launch G4GC as an organization, a major donor withdrew from the field, creating a gap of more than $40 million in annual giving to girls in North America.

By the early 2010s, the Men and Boys of Color donor collaborative, a philanthropic collaborative of men including heads of foundations and philanthropic-serving institutions whose goal was to mobilize resources to support the well-being of boys nationwide, had effectively mobilized tens of millions of dollars and a presidentially sanctioned effort to address the well-being of men and boys. In 2014, President Barack Obama launched his signature program My Brother's Keeper, which explicitly elevated men's and boys' issues. This program took center stage in philanthropic circles, often relegating girls and women to the margins. But I was clear that girls needed a similar investment.

Men's and boys' programming were robustly funded across the country, but the funding for women's and girls' initiatives was minuscule by comparison. President Barack Obama also created the White House Council on Women and Girls, which served as a powerful convener of organizations and thought leaders among girls-serving organizations nationwide, but there was no comparable philanthropic infrastructure to support it. The investments we make in boys are necessary, but they cannot be made to the exclusion of investments in girls and nonbinary or gender-expansive youth. We need a both/and strategy, and there are enough resources to achieve this.

As the CEO of G4GC, I would finally be in a position to make strategic decisions about how to leverage and grow resources to support girls across the country who were actively engaged in uplifting their homes, schools, communities, and other institutions. My vision for philanthropy is that it should function as a site of collective care. My vision is for what I call "our grandmothers' philanthropy." My maternal grandmother is from Texas, where her family cultivated the soil to grow the food they would eat and share with their community. When she moved to California, she brought this skill set with her. Some of my earliest memories are of her trading her fruits with other farmers in the area so they could collectively make meals to feed their families. One family had tomatoes and potatoes, another family had chickens and fruit trees, and another grew onions and garlic. Early on, I learned that if I have tomatoes and potatoes, and you have onions and apples, together, we will not starve.

I applied this philosophy to G4GC's Theory of Impact, which states:

> Coordinated acts of honoring the interconnectedness of our families and communities shape not only our understanding of how to best resource social movements, but also our ability to recognize direct-service by and for girls of Color as central to movement-building intended to transform outcomes in their communities. This legacy of ancestral philanthropy understands these components as nonlinear and not mutually exclusive.

In other words, our families teach us how to resource young people—and the practices of our communities inform how we understand the value of girls. By calling in an "ancestral philanthropy," I am inviting adults who work with and/or parent girls to embrace the ways of giving that have always operated outside of the *sector* of philanthropy. I'm inviting them to activate the care of our elders. I'm inviting them to activate the *knowing* that reveals that investing in girls is essential to the well-being of our society. Patriarchy obscures our ability to see our girls. In order to counter this erasure, our task is to unapologetically bring girls' voices into the room—and to stand in the gap for them when they can't be in the room. This was an important place to start the conversation about how to resource girls in our communities through an intersectional lens. Few foundations and even fewer individual donors work to develop an analysis about how to most effectively and robustly invest in girls, preferring instead to simply write a check. Indeed, girls have been an afterthought in philanthropic giving—and girls of color are even further removed from the center of conversations. This has to change. Visibility is power.

The challenge, of course, was launching G4GC at the beginning of a global pandemic. For months, communities, cities, and states across the nation were shut down in response to growing fears about the spread of the deadly COVID-19 virus. I was not new to building a virtual workspace, as I had previously founded and led NBWJI as a virtual institute. But I was tasked to grow a team and cultivate a giving strategy for girls of color in the midst of one of the deadliest times in human history. One thing was for certain—this was not work that could be done alone. Almost immediately, colleagues from my previous roles in research and advocacy sent me notes encouraging me to move resources in ways that were flexible, to operate with urgency, engage an intersectional lens, and lead with love. They encouraged me to lean into the activities that have always kept us safe and well, such as building out a community of trusted advisers and colleagues to support my journey, and developing a council of trusted partners to help. As the proverb says, "If you want to go fast, go alone; if you want to go far, go together."

I hired Maheen a few months into my tenure, and together we went on to build an organization that would eventually resource more than four hundred organizations across the country, in every state, along with Washington, D.C., Guam, and Puerto Rico. Moving resources in philanthropy, I learned, is less about how many checks one can write and more about how we can organize investments to grow the effective strategies that already exist in communities. These investments came from a wide range of resources, including philanthropic grants, loans, venture capital, etc. We invested in the activities and interventions that we knew worked. I set out to resource girls and movements that work with girls in a way that would add the least amount of stress to an already stressful scenario.

Mere months into the launch of G4GC, George Floyd and Breonna Taylor were both tragically murdered by law enforcement. The world, not just the nation, suddenly became privy to the egregious uses of force that too many law enforcement officers deploy against Black people. Protests took shape across the country. Murals and protest art sprang up almost everywhere. News articles and feature segments were established to interrogate the reach of the criminal legal system, and the state-sanctioned violence that people of African descent experience in the United States. Public and private entities reacted with an array of responses that promised to shift financial resources toward underserved communities, to strengthen their capacity for healing and justice. Google committed $50 million to Historically Black Colleges and Universities, JPMorganChase committed $30 billion to investments and loans—in all, America's fifty largest public companies and their foundations committed more than $50 billion in an unprecedented effort to acknowledge the need for a repair of the root causes of disparities and harm against Black people and other people of color in the United States.[1] Many of the largest and most high-profile corporations established Diversity, Equity, and Inclusion departments, portfolios, and infrastructures to suggest their commitment to these issues would be lasting. However, because the Diversity, Equity, and Inclusion conversation was so intertwined with racial justice, there was little public attention paid to the fact that gender justice efforts are included under the mantle of D.E.I. as well. Women in key diversity positions established in and before 2020 called on everyone within earshot to expand their investments in the well-being of historically marginalized groups to include our girls. Many philanthropic and investment strategies at the national level, such as G4GC's Black Girl Freedom Fund and the Southern Black Girls and Women's

Consortium's Black Girl Dream Fund, were explicitly intersectional to call attention to this fact.

It was an opportunity to explore the pandemic, which all of our young people were experiencing along with their older counterparts. But it was also an opportunity to explore the violence that young people experience at the intersections of their identities. Breonna Taylor was only twenty-six years old, and, as mentioned earlier in this book, the reason we even know about George Floyd is because of seventeen-year-old Darnella Frazier.

G4GC was in its nascent stage, but it was composed of people who had long been engaged in issues involving the well-being of girls and gender-expansive youth of color across the country. We may have been a young organization, but we were like a toddler with an "old soul." We were still learning how to walk in our current physical body, but our consciousness knew what needed to happen. We went to work, deploying grants and resources, and supporting the organizations in our ecosystem as best we could through technical assistance and organizational development.

We awarded more than $26 million in fewer than five years through a portfolio of four funds. The first fund I launched was the Love Is Healing COVID-19 Response Fund in 2020. Its main goal was to respond in real time to girls across the country in need of support for their exposure to the virus. But it also addressed the dearth of infrastructure across the country that was responding to the unique experiences and conditions of girls. At the time, there were hundreds of organizations providing direct services to girls throughout the U.S., but their efforts were uncoordinated; they weren't connected to each other in a way that would facilitate community and offer support for each other. There were only a handful of foundations that had an explicit focus on girls, and until G4GC formed, there was not a single foundation focused on resourcing movements and organizations that center the wisdom and well-being of girls of color. Later that year, we launched the Black Girl Freedom Fund as part of the #1billion4blackgirls campaign, a ten-year philanthropic initiative that I founded in partnership with Tarana Burke; LaTosha Brown; Fatima Goss Graves; Joanne Smith; feminist activist, scholar, and writer Salamishah Tillet; photographer and art therapist Scheherazade Tillet; and philanthropic leader Teresa Younger to mobilize a $1 billion investment in Black girls and gender-expansive youth by 2030. We enlisted the support of early architects of organized giving to Black girls, tapping the wisdom of founder and principal of Black Harvest Tynesha McHarris, longtime philanthropic advocate Nakisha Lewis, and others to amplify the fact that organizations centering Black girls are woefully underfunded. We knew then, as we know now, that when our girls are robustly resourced, the return exceeds our expectations. In 2021, G4GC launched the New Songs Rising Initiative for Indigenous Girls, a fund whose goal was to expand opportunities for Indigenous girls through grantmaking, convening, community building, mentorship, and peer support, with a specific emphasis on Indigenous cultural work. The fund also aimed to encourage the field of philanthropy to better meet the needs of Indigenous young people. We did this in partnership with the Seventh Generation Fund for Indigenous Peoples, one of the nation's oldest philanthropic organizations dedicated to Indigenous People's self-determination and the sovereignty of Native nations. In 2022, G4GC partnered with the Black Trans Fund, the first national fund dedicated to uplifting, resourcing, and building the capacity of Black trans social justice leaders, to launch the Holding a Sister Initiative, a fund dedicated to trans youth who identify as Black, Indigenous, Latine, Asian, Arab, Pacific Islander, and other people of color nationwide. This initiative mobilized funds and brought attention and resources to organizations that serve and are led by trans girls and youth of color. Another goal of this initiative was to hold space for cis and trans girls of color to build intentional solidarity with one another in efforts to advance racial and gender justice. Philanthropy and corporate giving were growing, and so was the number of women-led foundations and philanthropic-serving organizations (PSOs), which are intermediaries that solely focus to increase the capacity of foundations to operate with efficiency, care, and, in some cases, specificity.*

In addition to these philanthropic efforts, G4GC partnered with Second Muse Capital, a global company that works with public and private entities to design and manage impact investments that "finance economies of the future," to design a fund that would align with the investment priorities of our communities.[2] Launched as the Future Economy Lab to Abundantly Resource Girls and Gender Expansive Youth of Color, the project ultimately engaged more than four hundred girls and gender-expansive youth ages thirteen to twenty-four, including thirty-nine fellows, to participate in a research project that explored what was important to them, and how adults should invest time—and money—to best align with their values.

The research design portion of this project was more generative than we imagined. More girls and gender-expansive youth participated in the project than we originally anticipated. And their response to the question *What do economies that foster the well-being of girls of color and their communities look like?* produced a list of eighteen "catalytic factors" they thought should inform any plan to achieve economic justice. Their participation has helped philanthropy answer what it means to invest in nurturing the dreams, joy, and power of youth. Among the eighteen catalytic factors

* Philanthropic-serving organizations (PSOs) are organizations designed to lead, strengthen, inform, mobilize, and increase the capacity of the philanthropic sector to work more efficiently in specific geographic regions, identity-based networks, and topics.

identified by youth for investment are: "Rightful ownership of intellectual property, like artistic creations, and their proper credit; honoring all professions, trades, and vocations as valuable and respected; many active connections to role models of people like you; feelings of peacefulness in everyday life; and access to and value placed on diverse educational opportunities and career paths," among others.[3] Their contributions allow us to examine what young people in our communities considered important and to intentionally expand the underdeveloped public narrative about girls and gender-expansive youth. It was important for us to design something that demonstrated they could be more than just consumers. They can be more than cute. They can be entrepreneurs and inform entrepreneurship.

These girls and gender-expansive youth demonstrated a deep capacity for articulating their worth alongside their values and invited the adults to do the same. What we gained from the process of working with young people this closely is a heightened appreciation for how activating the radical imaginations of our youth can transform our understanding of what is possible. "Abundantly Investing in Girls, Femmes, and Gender Expansive Youth of Color," the summary report of findings we published, shared the young people's collective vision: "An abundant future is where we are consistently thriving in a tranquil world, surrounded by a sustainable society built on communal love reimagined, that is inclusive of all of us and our cultures."[4] What a vision! Our challenge is executing it.

In 2022, the U.S. Supreme Court rendered a decision on *Dobbs v. Jackson Women's Health Organization,* which overturned the ruling that federally protected reproductive freedoms established fifty years prior in *Roe v. Wade.* The court ruled that the Constitution does not confer a right to abortion and returned decision-making on the issue of abortion to each state. Writing for the majority opinion, Justice Alito stated, "In my judgment, on the issue of abortion, the Constitution is neither pro-life nor pro-choice. The Constitution is neutral, and this Court likewise must be scrupulously neutral. The Court today properly heeds the constitutional principle of judicial neutrality and returns the issue of abortion to the people and their elected representatives in the democratic process."[5] This meant that where a person lived would determine whether or not they would have access to a safe and legal abortion. This immediately impacted access to care for people of all ages who give birth, but especially those living in conservative states, where reproductive rights were routinely limited and often egregiously denied. While the majority of the focus was on women, girls and nonbinary birthing people were also caught in the crosshairs. Many of the young people in our orbit were forced to consider options that were not ideal for their optimal health. Beyond abortion, removing the federal protections created a vacuum in funding for reproductive rights, as many philanthropists were concerned about supporting efforts that could be interpreted as illegal. This meant that organizations supporting girls in their reproductive decisions across the country were abandoned in a critical moment. The climate started to shift around the desires and needs of women and girls, focusing almost exclusively on reproductive rights.

Meanwhile, there were many other individual and structural assaults on the well-being of girls and young women. As women and girls are overrepresented in the care economy—the configuration of paid and unpaid labor that includes day care, home health aide workers, and elder care, among others —they were also disproportionately negatively impacted by the COVID-19 pandemic and its economic aftermath. The Centers for Disease Control reported that sexual violence increased for teen girls at schools and during the lockdown, confirming that "the number of young girls forced into sex grew by nearly 200,000 in just two years."[6] Many girls and young women were also experiencing violence at the intersection of their identities. For example, in 2022, a twenty-eight-year-old man in New York went on a hate-filled rampage and violently attacked seven women and girls of Asian descent in two hours, many of the victims under the age of twenty-one.[7]

Then, in 2023, the U.S. Supreme Court issued another blow to equity efforts, one that continues to impact financial investments in girls and young women nationwide. Rendering its decision on *Students for Fair Admissions v. Harvard,* the court effectively banned affirmative action in access to higher education by disallowing the consideration of race in college admissions.[8] Claiming that the "tragic failure of this Court was its misinterpretation of the Reconstruction Amendments" following the "failure" of slavery and its progeny, Justice Clarence Thomas wrote that the U.S. Constitution was a "colorblind" instrument that enunciates "that all men are created equal, are equal citizens, and must be treated equally before the law."[9] Where do we locate girls in this analysis? Girls' erasure from this sentiment of equal treatment and protections is typical, historical, and, unfortunately, prevalent among the landscape of funding and financial investments that seek to remedy historical oppression and repression. This is true even as they stand to bear the brunt of the decision. As Justice Sonia Sotomayor wrote in her dissenting opinion, "Superficial colorblindness in a society that systematically segregates opportunity will cause a sharp decline in the rates at which underrepresented minority students enroll in our Nation's colleges and universities, turning the clock back and undoing the slow yet significant progress already achieved."[10]

This decision impacts the life trajectory of more than half of our nation's youth, and more than a quarter of our nation's girls.[11] Though wage disparities persist, women comprise a greater percentage than men of degree-earning young adults, a statistic that holds across racial groups.[12] However, among young women, racial disparities also persist, which means that young women of color will be disproportionately impacted by the decision. Data from the Class of 2028, the first class to be admitted since the decision, demonstrated a noticeable decline in the admissions rates for Black and Latine students, including among colleges that are highly selective. At the Massachusetts Institute of Technology, the percentage of Black students admitted dropped from 15 percent to 5 percent, and at the University of North Carolina, the number of Black students enrolled as first-year and transfer students dropped by more than 25 percent. The decline for Hispanic students was 7 percent.[13] As disturbing as these trends are, they weren't the only consequence of the decision.

This Court's decision in *SFFA v. Harvard* was widely interpreted as granting permission for corporations—who made lofty promises in 2020 about their commitments to racial and gender justice—to retrench. In so doing, these corporations undermined efforts that were already under way to design an infrastructure for sustainable change nationwide. For example, many nonprofit organizations, especially smaller organizations working with girls who operate under the radar of philanthropy's largest institutions, received the public declarations to fund direct services to girls and gender-expansive youth as an invitation to grow their institutions, by increasing staffing and the scope of the programming work they took on. Many of the nation's smallest organizations tend to operate with only one or two staff members, sometimes working without a salary or other infrastructure necessities that support the sustainability of organizations. Almost immediately, efforts to advance equity came to a halt. Women who had decision-making power for D.E.I. efforts were fired or replaced. Corporations underwent immediate restructures, laying off staff and rescinding the financial resources that were put in place in 2020. Efforts to "diversify workforces, help ensure equity in hiring and promotion practices, and create a more inclusive organizational culture" were abandoned and promises that were made for funding were not honored.[14] Corporations began to liberally interpret the Supreme Court's decision to end affirmative action to mean that all of their racially conscious and/or explicit efforts to advance racial and gender equity were unconstitutional. This retrenchment had devastating effects on girls across the nation.

Almost immediately, the promised investments began to disappear. Following the Supreme Court ruling, more than a dozen attorneys general issued letters that threatened legal action for corporate diversity efforts.[15] The climate shifted almost immediately in a fearful, anticipatory anxiety for what might come next. Leadership positions in D.E.I. were eliminated and programs toppled in the public and private sectors across the nation.[16] I even attended meetings where conservative leaders of industry were emboldened to challenge the value of D.E.I. programming. I remember the feeling of anger that began to form inside of me as the CEO of a major financial institution sat proudly in a private room, where I was one of a few women and only two Black women in attendance, and repeatedly emphasized how "not woke" he was, in order to garner the trust of other corporate leaders. Of course, he lost mine—but did that even matter to him?

That's a rhetorical question. We all know the answer.

Philanthropy was also swirling with memos and conversations about how the Supreme Court decision impacted investments in communities that faced historical—and continuous—marginalization across the nation. The stiff arm encountered by many of us who advocate for girls in economic spaces was brutal, while the already tiny investment in girls became even smaller, and devastatingly so for girls of color. Organizations that were explicitly focused on girls, particularly girls of color, were especially vulnerable given that their acknowledgment of race was viewed as an automatic disqualifier for funding. Some high-profile philanthropists made significant statements about the importance of investing in women's issues, especially given that we were on the precipice of the most significant wealth transfer in history. For example, in a statement justifying her commitment to more than $1 billion to advance the power of women, Melinda French Gates, philanthropist and founder of Pivotal Ventures, stated, "decades of research on economics, wellbeing, and governance make it clear that investing in women and girls benefits everyone."[17] By 2030, women will inherit much of the $30 trillion passed on by the "baby boomer" generation. This is a transfer of wealth that comes with more than just money; it's been called "the power shift of the century."[18]

We are essentially at a crossroads of convergent realities—on the one hand, women and girls have more power than ever before as decision-makers regarding investments and the stewardship of financial resources, and on the other, the retrenchments in giving and investment are more specific and insidious, threatening to undermine their access to key public and private-sector leadership positions. These conversations are exhausting, primarily because they are never operating in a vacuum. As an organization working with girls-serving organizations across the country, G4GC held a series of conversations with organizations in our ecosystem that acknowledged the harm perpetrated by the philanthropic sector by shifting funding so abruptly, and invited their thoughts about strategizing for the future. Our organizational value of transparency and leading with love required us to be in community with these courageous and committed leaders of organizations, rather than shy away from our mission at one of the most critical times for investment in our nation's history. Still, it was tough—really tough. Approximately 90 percent of our ecosystem was effectively defunded or experiencing a devastating retrenchment in funding. How could we feel good about conversations with the last to be funded about how they became the first line item cut?

First calls are almost always the hardest. Fear of the unknown can sometimes allow us to create a story that isn't true or that is exaggerated. As the CEO, I walked into these calls with a great deal of sadness. Therapy taught me to acknowledge these feelings. So many of the women I know across sectors and disciplines, especially those of us who have committed our lives to shining a light on those experiencing the deepest wounds our society administers, pretend we're okay when we are not. I have come to learn that leading with integrity also means being honest about where it hurts. Our community of warriors on behalf of girls was suffering—we were *all* suffering.

As I sat down for the first call with women across the country, I reached for my notebook so that I could take notes during the meeting. When I did, a postcard slipped out and fell by my feet. I glanced at it and immediately began to smile. Months earlier, I'd bought a postcard that featured an image of Alice Walker in 1976, captured by photographer Bernard Gotfryd. In the image, she is looking straight into the camera, a soft and curly Afro framing her face as she confidently shares a knowing smile. I love this photo so much because it reminds me that we have the audacity to be encouraged, to be forceful, to be powerful . . . even when others don't know we exist. On the back of the postcard, I had scribbled in black ink one of my favorite quotes from her, words you may recognize as the epigraph for this book:

> *We will never have to be other than who we are in order to be successful. We realize that we are, ourselves, unlimited, and our experiences valid. It is for the rest of the world to recognize this, if they choose.*
>
> —Alice Walker

We are the thing we need to actualize the abundance we know is possible. We are, ourselves, unlimited. It was exactly the reminder I needed.

* * *

A signature program of G4GC's Black Girl Freedom Fund is Black Girl Freedom Week. It is a weeklong dedication to Black girls during Black History Month, intended to share their brilliance with the public. As a cofounder of the initiative, I have been involved with this celebration since 2021. The weeklong engagement has provided a platform for Black girls and gender-expansive youth to share their perspectives on a host of issues—from safety to beauty to politics—and has created a virtual space for adults to hear directly from these young people about what is on their minds. Occurring during the week in which Black feminist writer Audre Lorde and celebrated novelist Toni Morrison were born, Black Girl Freedom Week has been an opportunity to ground ourselves in the wisdom of Black girl and femme voices. The week has attracted a cross section of leaders from the arts, academia, corporate leadership, and other sectors, including the #1billion-4blackgirls cofounders, actor/producer Rashida Jones, actors Tracee Ellis Ross, Kelly McCreary, and Sanaa Lathan, director Gina Prince-Bythewood, financial executive Georgette "Gigi" Dixon, political strategist Stephanie Brown James, philanthropist Yvonne Moore, and others.

In 2023, I launched the week in partnership with two young people who have been part of our G4GC community since our inception. Sydnie Chandler Monet (she/her), a student, entrepreneur, and CEO of Perfect Timing Podcast, joined me, as well as Jamison Ford (s/he, them), a student, orator, youth activist, and humanitarian, who has been part of G4GC's participatory grant-making efforts.

"Hi, everyone! I'm Sydnie Chandler Monet," Sydnie said in her typical perky tone. "I'm an entrepreneur, motivational speaker, and host and CEO of Perfect Timing Podcast."

Sydnie makes me proud. She is a young person who realized early that her dream of hosting a podcast that centers on issues of importance to girls was not only possible but within her reach. I met her when she was just fifteen years old. At that point, her podcast was just taking off, and she was working, with the support of her dedicated mother, to position herself as an emergent voice in the sea of podcasts. Several of her podcast episodes have been featured in Elite Conversations' Top 10 Podcasts.

"Hey y'all, I'm Jamison Ford," they said in a smooth, Southern drawl. "A philanthropist and revolutionary."

I could feel my heart swell at that introduction. The smile that immediately spread across my face proved difficult to hide.

For a young person to call themselves a "philanthropist"—and understand what that means—doesn't just happen. It takes a lot of investment and care, especially if those young people are not from families that hold generational wealth. It requires doing the work to educate young people about decision-making processes in philanthropy, helping them reconcile their own relationships with money, and understanding the criteria used to determine whether a project or organization is one they want to invest in. Philanthropy is defined as "the desire to promote the welfare of others, expressed especially by the generous donation of money to good cause," but its roots are simply actions taken to amplify a "love of humanity."[19]

Participatory grantmaking is the practice of shared decision-making when awarding grants. Typically, it involves a group of people not hired by a foundation or other grantmaking institution being tasked with reading proposals and being in discussion with the grantmaking institution's staff about which organization(s) should receive monetary awards. In the philanthropic sector, participatory grantmaking can take shape in a host of ways. It can include a committee of readers being tasked with sharing their recommendations to a program officer, who then makes the case to the board for final decision-making. It can include a consensus project between communities and professionals in the philanthropic sector, where a series of meetings produce recommendations to an executive or board for final approval. What has made G4GC's participatory grantmaking efforts unique is our commitment to engage the voices of young people throughout the year, not only when grants are being considered. What also differentiates our efforts from others is that we take on the responsibility to perform the due diligence *before* young people review the portfolios, so when they make decisions about which organizations should receive funding, those decisions are final. This not only enables these young people to feel empowered to make the decisions they determined were necessary to improve the lives of girls and gender-expansive youth, it also gives us an opportunity to demonstrate to them how much we value their opinions about work that affects them. This is action-oriented, trust-based philanthropy in practice. We are creating the conditions to holistically resource girls' well-being. When we invest holistically, we foster freedom. When girls are free, they can imagine and create rules that benefit not only themselves but all of us.

This is bigger than youth-based work, and it is bigger than participatory decision-making. It is both, and that is what makes the contributions of G4GC necessary. This work to resource organizations centering the wisdom and well-being of girls and femmes requires financial investments that are grounded in all of the ways we invest beyond money. This was one of the lessons from my research on school discipline and advocacy efforts to end pushout. Addressing the pushout of girls required us to examine dress code policies and other codes of conduct that revealed biases against other groups as well. Unfair hair regulations keeping students from wearing locs, colored braids, or extensions that were impacting girls also impacted boys, particularly Indigenous and Black boys, who may wear hair in longer styles for cultural reasons. Clothing regulations that disproportionately affected girls also affected nonbinary youth, who are often targeted for citations associated with wearing clothes that align with their gender identity even if it does not align with their gender assignment at birth. Ending the "Slap Ass Fridays," discussed earlier in this book, not only made middle school girls safer in the Bay Area, it improved the quality of the learning environment for everyone, but especially young people who are fighting against the harmful, dangerous elements of patriarchy that excuse abhorrent behavior as just "boys being boys." Instituting language and practices to make dress code policies more equitable reduces the risk of scanning and policing the bodies of our children in ways that can trigger those who are survivors of violence. Investing the time to more deeply interrogate school-based practices for their impact on girls creates opportunities to make the learning space more equitable to everyone. Again, the work with girls is *generative,* not extractive; and therein lies the possibility for healing.

G4GC's approach to participatory grantmaking is a combination of all of the elements essential to investing in girls with more than money. We activate girls' *knowing* and educate them about the structures and processes they have capacity to influence as decision–makers. These activities elevate their wisdom and acknowledge their experiential learning and interests. We ensure that girls have access to information relevant to their decision-making while ensuring their emotional well-being. Girls and gender-expansive youth who participate in our projects have access to therapists and others who can support their wellness along the journey. Our fellowship programs come with access to a professional who can provide guidance and counsel. Therapists affiliated with our programs help to navigate young people's relationships with money and with conditions such as poverty and gender-based violence that can prevent girls from realizing their purpose in this world.

Professionals working in the philanthropic sector must not lose sight of the tremendous opportunities we have to invest in all of the ways that ensure the well-being of our girls. When girls are well, they pour into others in their communities, so investing in girls leads to our collective liberation. Only 2 percent of philanthropic giving goes to women and girls across the country. Less than 1 percent of philanthropic giving goes to women and girls of color, with Black women and girls receiving approximately just 0.5 percent.[20] The disproportionately low level of giving to girls suggests an underappreciation for the value of investments in our girls. Much of this gap can be attributed to a distortion of how girls experience philanthropy, and their visibility across the sector. I have observed this to manifest in a few primary ways.

1. The adultification of girls in our grantmaking and giving strategies. Grantmakers and private donors often assume that by giving to women's issues, it will trickle down to girls. But that is not true. Funding directed to women's issues is granted to women-serving organizations, and while it may also benefit the children of women, if that is an organizational focus, we cannot assume that by investing in women, we are investing in girls.
2. The erasure of girls' power-building strategies. While adultification informs the strategy of philanthropy when it comes to engaging with girls, their portfolio priorities often infantilize and/or diminish investments, because girls are perceived as "cute." As Maheen and I often share, being seen as "cute" results in girls receiving "cute" money, or small amounts. Girls are often treated simply as consumers of programs or participants, rather than leaders and agents of change in the organizations and institutions that benefit the larger society.
3. "Trust-based philanthropy" is an emergent framework within the philanthropic sector to shift the power dynamic and relationship between those who resource

nonprofit organizations, and those who receive those funds. The movement is intended to facilitate "mutual accountability between funders and nonprofits" by building trust and collaboration, rather than control, compliance, and directives.[21] However, "trust-based philanthropy" often practices saviorism and patriarchal models that cause more damage than they do good. The saviorism manifests as foundations and other philanthropic sources seeking to do more than just "write a check," still wielding power in ways that show they assume they possess the "best practice" remedy to a social problem. This influence is sometimes manifested via priorities created without consultation with impacted communities, or funding streams and structures that still only provide resources via institutional grants, which makes some of our girls' more innovative approaches to problem solving ineligible for resources. The patriarchal model is reflected when philanthropic organizations design resourcing organizations using models that foster competition (for example, through requests for proposals) instead of collaboration and partnership (for example, through nominations and relationship building to discover existing relationships within a community).

Rather than emphasizing the development of relationships that allow leaders in the philanthropic sector to consider behaviors and values that encourage communities to trust philanthropy, "trust-based" efforts often prioritize the vantage point of the foundation or granting institution. This ignores centuries of structural harms that produced the wealth now being regranted and centers instead only on the perspectives of the wealthy. This also

> diminishes the potential to talk about how institutions build trust with our girls. To *cede* power—to release the control over the stewardship of resources to girls—provides opportunities for philanthropic institutions to *seed* power among our girls, honoring their wisdoms, priorities, and strategies for improving the conditions and environments in which they will grow.

When philanthropic organizations do not robustly invest in girls, we do ourselves a disservice. Girls grow into adults who will continue to shape the landscape of our communities and many of its core institutions. Marginalizing girls' issues or regarding them as "niche" undermines efforts to build whole and healthy communities. Therefore, adults should intentionally locate girls in the U.S. in the global conversations about girls' well-being. Once we've done that, we need to make financial decisions that align with what we find.

I asked Jody Myrum, long-standing philanthropic organizer and founder and director of Our Collective Practice, an organization that seeks to "drive change through collaborations with funders, policy makers, activists, culture change makers, artists, and practitioners who work with and for girls across the world," about how we also make connections with global movements of girls, and why this is important.[22] She shared, "It' s important to create spaces of connection, of solidarity between the work. Because not only are the issues connected, but the solutions are connected."

Girls in the U.S. are often treated as outliers compared to girls' plight in other countries. However, when data are disaggregated by race, gender, ability, and other conditions, we see that many of the girls in the U.S. experience levels of harm that are commensurate with girls in developing countries. It's time we not only see girls as being in need of our financial investments in the U.S. but connect them with their sisters in other lands so as to build the type of cross-national learnings and alliances that can support their well-being. Solidarity increases visibility, and in matters of philanthropy, visibility is power.

"We should invest in girls, first and foremost, because they deserve better," Jody continued. "They deserve to be safe, to be free, to play, the space to dream, to make mistakes, to have choices, and to just be whatever that means to them. This is their right, and they deserve it. We also know that girls are at the forefront of sparking, leading, and participating in every social justice movement that exists in the world today and historically. They are transforming systems and responding to emergencies—and they are doing all of this with brave and creative strategies, and with such deep political clarity that is unique and distinct from their older adult allies. In addition to them deserving better, if we do not invest in them, we will not get to the democracies or justice we need. We will not get to freedom, to safety, and to lives of dignity for everyone. Because the worlds girls are dreaming of, and actively building through their activism, are worlds that are life-affirming for everyone."

The political sophistication that girls display in programming often floats under the radar of large philanthropic organizations, corporate giving strategies, and family foundations, so they allocate minimal resources to specifically grow these efforts. Programming is interpreted often as an enrichment exercise, rather than the power-building exercise that we know it to be. At G4GC and among our other colleagues in philanthropy who work with girls, we have discovered that working with girls and gender-expansive youth is one of the fastest and most efficient ways to realize the futures we imagine. As poet Nikki Giovanni said to me during our recorded interview about why we invest in girls, "It's a good idea."

"It's important that we [funders] match their creativity, their bravery, their boldness, their political clarity, and move abundant resources to them," Jody continued. "We need to be moving a lot more resources to them—and better resources; resources that match and reflect the kinds of organizing they're doing, the work that they're doing. I'm talking about moving resources in ways that are both broad and wide. So, that's centering girls in all of our movements, all of our sectors, all of our funding strategies, whether it's climate justice, economic justice, disability justice, education, racial justice, or whatever the entry point. Whatever the movement or sector that funders are working on, we need to be centering girls because they are impacted by these struggles and they are also at the forefront of responding to them."

I often say that every issue is a girls' issue, so it's important for us to locate and resource them in all domains of public life, explicitly. Not in a trickle-down strategy that assumes funding will eventually reach them. Move the resources to them directly, and to the organizations that are working with them directly, to activate the conditions we want to see in the world.

"In the context of a broader global movement," Jody continued, "we are working towards the freedom and liberation of all people in ways that center girls. The experiences girls face might look different on the surface, across different contexts, but they are caused by the same forms of oppression and white supremacy, colonialism, and patriarchy. We need to address these root causes that put all girls at risk of violence and discrimination. Girls know this well. When you talk to girls about solidarity, they often talk about the struggles of girls in other contexts and they have deep clarity that they will not be free if girls in other countries and contexts are not. And yet, most of the time, funders insist on separating girls in the U.S. from girls outside of the U.S., but the issues that impact girls in the U.S. are not different than the issues that impact girls outside of the U.S. Funders need to change their strategies, because this is not effective. It will not create the change we need for girls or for anyone."

Philanthropic efforts must better understand that our world is now connected in ways that force us to reimagine what it means to abundantly resource our girls. The artificial and now arbitrary ways in which funders silo grantmaking to resource around only a single issue, or a single region, is an antiquated model that undermines our ability to forge the international sisterhood and siblingship that will liberate us all.

Maheen and I were in Seattle one fall, meeting over breakfast, preparing for an event that we were attending that evening. After checking in, strategizing, and venting about some other thorns, we laughed about how we manage to stay in this work despite the land mines.

"Why?" I asked her. "Why do you stay in it?"

"Because of a fourteen-year-old girl I met in Alameda County juvenile hall," she said. "She was the first girl that I met there. I asked her why she was inside, and she said, 'I'm charged with arson.' So, I asked what happened."

That is always the right, trauma-informed, and healing responsive question: What happened?

"She said, 'They say that I burned down my group home,'" Maheen continued. "Then she looked at me and asked, 'Do you believe that I could burn down my group home?' and I could see in her face that she was testing me to see how I was receiving and perceiving her. So, I said, 'Well, why would you do that?' And she said, 'They weren't giving us toilet paper. They weren't giving us toothbrushes. They had locks on the fridge and I got frustrated, so I lit a match and it fell into a trash can.'"

As Maheen told the story, I had flashbacks to the many group homes and residential correctional facilities I'd been in over the years, where children told similar stories of scarcity, abuse, agitation, and thus anger.

"For me, in that moment," Maheen continued, "what I recognized in her was a very righteous rage and a frustration that she and her peers were not getting their material needs met, and a resourcefulness to say, 'I have nothing else to do but to burn this down.' Her sense of injustice was so great. Now, I'm not saying that she actually did that, or not, but the fact that she didn't care what happened on the other side of that says a lot."

I nodded, very familiar with those types of interactions and the feeling it evokes in those of us who love our girls and fight against their mistreatment. Girls with the fewest resources are often the ones who imagine the best for all of us. They know the pain of being left out of the vision, and they often imagine inclusive worlds, rather than exclusionary ones. Adults should be careful not to clip their wings by cutting off opportunities or discouraging them from taking advantage of resources before they take off, because these are the young people who challenge conventional notions of leadership and investment. Girls invite adults to consider power as a collective tool, rather than as an agent of oppression. They rally our spirits, not just our hearts and minds—and that's a gift. That's giving.

"I think so much about the power and the promise that lives inside group homes, in the streets, and in cells," Maheen said. "That girl is so important to why I do this. I recognized that if I cared about human rights, if I cared about justice, if I cared about the girl that was inside me, I had to figure out ways to honor girls now. She's still in my life, and she has managed to survive and be an extraordinary mother. She's still on a journey but that's because she never got the resources that she deserved. Things are still hard for her, and they don't have to be. Had she been able to get resources, things would have shifted for her and her daughters."

Maheen is right. Our work is fundamentally about shifting the lives of our girls because they are worthy—and making investments that are meaningful and transformative. Economic parity for girls and women at large is at stake. The physical and mental health of generations is at stake. Lives are at stake.

"Stories like these are the reason why we're in philanthropy right now," Maheen continued. "There are so many ways and so many points of entry around this conversation of how we respond to young people. Girls we know hold these deeply important roles in community, and their families and institutions. We've done advocacy in other spaces around these issues, but we absolutely still hold relationships with young folks . . . Why did *you* go into philanthropy?"

"Hmmm, why *did* I go into philanthropy?" I paused for dramatic effect to think for a moment, and then we laughed. "I went into philanthropy because for me, it felt like the next iteration of my work. I had spent all these years asking for there to be something concrete that could respond to girls' needs. I wanted to build an institution that functions in alignment with the values and unique nature of how giving could transform lives, especially girls' lives and girls of color's lives."

"For me, it goes back to our organizer roots that are about relationship building," Maheen said. "It is about making a case for girls. For me, impacting the material lives of the people who have raised me in the work, impacting the young people who are in the work now, and being able to actually put cash in their pockets so that they can expand what is possible for them . . . yes, that feels like the place I'm supposed to be."

That's what I meant when I wrote about our grandmothers' philanthropy. Maheen was speaking it to life.

"In my core, I believe that our world will eventually actualize justice for our girls," Maheen continued. "When our movements and people that come from girls' work are robustly resourced, I know we'll get there."

* * *

The investments I propose in this chapter and the other chapters are foundational to the landscape of investments that produce liberated futures for our girls. The measure of our success is not the extent to which girls' issues are visible enough to warrant our attention. What's important is the extent to which our investments in these other issues locate and address the needs of girls alongside other more routinely named populations impacted by social policy or business decisions. To reach these young people, we have to engage bold strategies that challenge us to consider the whole human we are seeking to invest in, rather than the trope or stereotype that guides so much of our current decision-making and understanding of girlhood nationwide and globally. Making the investment in girls is to resource them to reach their full potential. If we consider all of the different ways that we pour into our young people, all of the different ways that could inspire them to lead a next generation movement for justice and well-being, we would be able to reach every child, even those that Bertice mentioned, who "fall through the cracks."

If we really commit to resourcing our girls with money and more, we will transform our thoughts and align our actions to create conditions for their well-being, not just their survival, and that is how we, ourselves, become unlimited.

AFTERWORD:
Activating a S.A.C.R.E.D. and L.O.V.E.D. Worldview

I used to dream radical dreams
of blowing everyone away
with my perceptive powers
of correct analysis . . .

then I awoke and dug
that if I dreamed natural
dreams of being a natural
woman doing what a woman

does when she's natural

*I would have a revolution.**

This is an excerpt from one of my favorite poems by Nikki Giovanni. In it, she calls on women to consider the transformative power of being a woman. I somehow knew that Dr. Nikki was right the moment I read that poem. I quoted a portion of this poem in my senior portrait when I graduated from Columbia, imprinting its importance in my development, but its meaning crystallized for me after I gave birth to my firstborn, Ebony, in 2001. I was elated to discover that my body could do incredible things and host the creation of

* Nikki Giovanni, "Revolutionary Dreams," 1974.

life. Birthing is, indeed, a miracle. I often call Ebony a "new soul," because her eyes take in everything and process life as if it is all a wonder, as if she's seeing it all for the first time. Weeks after coming into this world, she would wake up in the middle of the night seeking food and refreshment, as babies do. Her little round face was framed by the natural wrap of her hair. Her lips pursed, and her eyes wide, she would carefully scan the room, seemingly searching for focus and familiarity. I believe it's one of the traits that made her such a powerful visual artist later in life.

"We're your family, baby," I would say softly. "She's okay . . ."

And then I would kiss her, because, of course, she was the most beautiful being I had ever seen. She was an extension of life that I didn't know was possible, and it was then that I clearly understood that I would do everything in my power to create conditions that were as conducive as possible to happiness, fulfillment, and freedom for her. As parents do, I fell deeply in love with my baby—and that meant I wanted to facilitate spaces that would be safe and healing for her, her sister, and, later, every other girl that comes to life on Earth. Making life better for her and other girls does not mean that life is never challenging. It means that we intentionally locate girls in efforts to improve our society such that our actions do not *intentionally* trip her because of biases and structural barriers to her success. Through Ebony, a new world of possibility opened to me. She taught me the meaning of loving our girls unconditionally and moving with an appreciative inquiry of how to protect her and other girls from victimization and abuse. She was the invitation I needed to reconnect with my seven-year-old self and begin to love her unconditionally as well. Through motherhood, I discovered what it means to do what a woman does naturally and have a revolution.

My invitation for people to engage with girls as "sacred and loved" is a path to explore ways of aligning our actions toward the goal of our girls being free. To invest in our daughters like they matter, consider "sacred and loved" as a guiding acronym for the specific actions and frameworks to help make this a reality.

S.A.C.R.E.D. & L.O.V.E.D.

See her. See her promise. See her purpose.

Actively challenge stereotypes and tropes that prevent personal connections.

Create opportunities for her leadership across circumstances, industries, and sectors.

Respond to her dysregulation with care.

Engage the mystic, encourage her to trust her intuition.

Dismantle structural barriers to her success.

&

Leverage your networks to invest in her economic advancement.

Optimize conditions for her mental and physical health. Let her play.

Value her with a spirit of abundance–there is enough. And so is she.

Educate and mentor her with the highest quality.

Declare her as a priority.

Sacred and loved. Our sacred inquiry is so much richer than the finite value of money. Let's act accordingly.

APPENDIX A: BLACK GIRL BILL OF RIGHTS*

We, Black girls, women, and gender-expansive youth deserve the right to exist with love, care, and a commitment to our needs. We stand united in our desire to be affirmed and celebrated in our Blackness in our communities and on every institutional and systemic level.

Every Black girl deserves:

- The right to education and information about African and Black history
- The right to express our blackness however we defines it without judgment
- The right to be safe and have our physical, emotional, and mental health honored, protected, and nurtured
- The right to real sex education, contraception, tampons, and pads
- The right to agency and control over our own bodies in every space

* The Black Girl Bill of Rights was first presented April 9, 2016, in New York City during the workshop "Our Declaration of Freedom and Humanity," which was facilitated by Sisters in Strength (Girls for Gender Equity) at *Black Girls Movement Conference 2016.* See: *https://natagenda4blackgirls.org/black-girls-bill-of-rights/*

- The right to justice and reparations
    - in response to harm and sexual assault
    - when police officers murder people of color
- The right to play and have fun
- The right to community, sisterhood, and support from other girls
- The right to BE—exactly who we are, free from stereotypes and insecurity, our full unique selves

APPENDIX B: 18 CATALYTIC FACTORS FOR INVESTING IN GIRLS AND GENDER-EXPANSIVE YOUTH OF COLOR*

According to the study, "a catalytic factor (a) has high network reach, or influences a high percentage of the network [girls and gender-expansive youth of color], (b) directly influences a lot of other factors, and (c) isn't influenced, itself, by many factors. **All three** of these characteristics, **in balance**, must be true for a factor to have a high probability of transforming the system."

1. Rightful ownership of intellectual property, like artistic creations, and their proper credit.
2. Honoring all professions, trades, and vocations as valuable and respected.
3. Many active connections to role models of people like you.
4. Feelings of peacefulness in everyday life.
5. Access to and value placed on diverse educational opportunities and career paths.
6. Reduction of everyday trauma like gun violence,

* From SecondMuse Capital and G4GC's *Abundantly Investing in Girls, Femmes, and Gender Expansive Youth of Color: Summary of Findings* (2023), pp. 6–8.

climate anxiety, gender-based violence and harassment, etc.

7. Redesign of governments, including Tribal and Native governments, for self-rule by diverse people protecting communities of color.
8. Informed, uplifting, community centered, and not harmful use of social media.
9. Feeling respected in public spaces for who you are.
10. Understanding and accepting the nuances of in-the-moment consent and behavior for violence prevention.
11. A loving relationship with the environment to foster self-healing.
12. Investment in and implementation of economic strategies that are not rooted in capitalism and consumerism.
13. Access to and use of a wide variety of well-resourced activities to demonstrate skills, attainment, expertise in and out of school.
14. Recognition and ready access to loving and compassionate spaces and networks for support.
15. Society's values shift toward the collective, the planet, and to reciprocal and healing interactions with the natural world.
16. Commitment to actively questioning and breaking down white supremacist norms and culture.
17. Access to immigration support focused on girls, femmes, and gender expansive youth of color.
18. On-the-spot access to language translation support in schools, hospitals, stores, etc., for girls, femmes, and gender-expansive youth of color.

ACKNOWLEDGMENTS

Giving honor to the Creator, I would like to extend my gratitude and appreciation for God's grace, guidance, and covering. I know that my emergence from some of life's most challenging moments is because of a greater force—a greater Love—more powerful than my own. I acknowledge the commitment, labor, joy, and magical healing abilities of ancestors who fought for gender equity, and I celebrate the growing cadre of people across age, gender, and racial identities who still demand that girls are treated as full and equal human beings worthy of investment.

No book is written alone, especially one like this, which draws upon decades of experiences and conversations. Thank you, family, friends, and partners in this work to elevate the well-being of girls at the intersections of their identities. I would especially like to thank my daughters—Ebony and Mahogany—for allowing me to reflect so openly in this book about their journeys in relation to the larger project of gender justice. To Marlon Smith, thank you for speaking life into me the way only you can.

To the people mentioned in and/or interviewed for this book, thank you for trusting me to share your wisdom and contributions. As always, a special shoutout to my agent Marie Brown for challenging me to tell more of my own story—and to my editor zakia henderson-brown and the team at The New Press for publishing this story! To the G4GC staff, board, co-investors, grantee partners, and full ecosystem, thank you for your commitment to our girls. Even in hostile climates, we will prevail. As Mary

McLeod Bethune reminded us, "Without faith, nothing is possible. With it, nothing is impossible."

Finally, I dedicated this book to Allison R. Brown, a friend, colleague, attorney, advocate, and philanthropic leader. Allison was a "real one" who was taken from this Earth before many of us were ready, but she left this gentle reminder: "Mothering is a privilege." I look back on our many conversations about our children and educational equity with fondness and appreciation. I lovingly offer this book in her memory.

NOTES

Introduction

1. For the purposes of this book, I use several terms in reference to the gender identity of young people. I use "girl/s" and "young women," though not interchangeably, to refer to any young person under the age of twenty-five who identifies as female. In this book, girls and young women may identify along the gender spectrum (i.e., cis, trans, nonbinary, gender-nonconforming, or gender-expansive) or sexuality continuum (i.e., heterosexual and LGBQIA+).

2. A. Dennis, "Nikki Giovanni's Moments for the Culture: A Talk with James Baldwin and Her 'Thug Life' Tattoo," Knoxnews.com, June 1, 2023, https://www.knoxnews.com/in-depth/news/2023/06/01/nikki-giovanni-top-cultural-moments-james-baldwin-tupac-tattoo/70219239007/.

3. G4GC [Grantmakers for Girls of Color]. *In Conversation with Nikki Giovanni: The Power of Imagination* [video], 2023.

4. Kimberlé Crenshaw, "Demarginalizing the Intersection of Race and Sex: A Black Feminist Critique of Antidiscrimination Doctrine, Feminist Theory and Antiracist Policies," *The University of Chicago Legal Forum* 1989, no. 1 (1989): 139–67.

5. Moya Bailey and Trudy, "On Misogynoir: Citation, Erasure, and Plagiarism," *Feminist Media Studies* 18, no. 4 (2018): 762–68, https://doi.org/10.1080/14680777.2018.1447395.

6. G4GC refers to "girl[s] of color" as any cis, trans, gender-expansive, nonbinary, and/or any girl- or femme-identified person aged twenty-five and younger who identifies as Black, Indigenous, Latina/e, Asian, Arab, Pacific Islander, and/or other people of color. For the purposes of this book, "girl" refers to any young person who identifies as female or femme.

1. *Knowing* Is Girls' Superpower

1. Girls are not only listening to the signals in their schools and homes that suggest that occupations and interests are gendered, but they also interpret them in their own activities and understandings of what is possible for them. When girls as young as age six digest gendered notions of intelligence, with only boys being "really, really smart," it means that they are less likely to pursue interests in fields commonly associated with intellectual achievement. See Lin Bian, Sarah Jane Leslie, and Andrei Cimpian, "Gender Stereotypes about Intellectual Ability Emerge Early and Influence Children's Interests," *Science* 355, no. 6323 (January 2017): 389–91, https://www.science.org/doi/10.1126/science.aah6524.

2. African American Policy Forum, https://www.aapf.org/.

3. Monique W. Morris (Couvson), "Race, Gender and the School to Prison Pipeline: Expanding Our Discussion to Include Black Girls," *African American Policy Forum,* 2012. Available at https://youthrex.com/wp-content/uploads/2019/02/Morris-Race-Gender-and-the-School-to-Prison-Pipeline.pdf.

4. *Revolutionary Dreaming* (2025). See: https://therevolutionarydreamingzine.

5. Ibid.

6. Justice for Black Girls, 2025. See: https://www.justiceforblackgirls.com/mission.

7. The Committee on African American Parity of the Human Rights Commission of San Francisco, *The Unfinished Agenda: The Economic Status of African Americans in San Francisco 1964–1990* (February 1993), https://media.api.sf.gov/documents/The_Unfinished_Agenda..._1.pdf.

8. *San Francisco NAACP v. San Francisco Unified School District,* https://clearinghouse.net/case/9939/.

9. L. Porter, M. Vazquez Cano, and I. Umansky, *Bilingual Education and America's Future: Evidence and Pathways* (Los Angeles, CA: The Civil Rights Project/Proyecto Derechos Civiles, UCLA, 2023).

10. Ofelia Garcia and Li Wei, "Translanguaging," in *The Encyclopedia of Applied Linguistics* online (2019), https://ofeliagarciadotorg.wordpress.com/wp-content/uploads/2019/05/garcialiweiappliedlinguistics.

11. Vivian E. Presiado and Brittany L. Frieson, "'Make Sure You See This': Counternarratives of Multilingual Black Girls' Language and Literacy Practices," *Literacy Research: Theory, Method, and Practice* 70 (2021): 388–407, at p. 389.

12. Ibid. See also E. Richardson, "'To Protect and Serve': African American Female Literacies," *College Composition and Communication* 53, no. 4 (2002): 675–704, https://doi.org/10.2307/1512121.

13. CEPR is a nonprofit, independent pan-European policy think tank. For

more on this study, see L. Bursztyn, A. Cappelen, et al., "How Gender Norms Are Perceived Across the World," June 29, 2023, https://cepr.org/voxeu/columns/how-gender-norms-are-perceived-across-world.

14. Ibid.

15. See David Sadker and Karen Zittleman, *Still Failing at Fairness: How Gender Bias Cheats Girls and Boys in School and What We Can Do About It* (Simon & Schuster, 2017).

16. Girls Leadership, *Ready to Lead* (2020), 20.

17. Ibid., 5.

18. Girls Leadership, *Why We Lead: Understanding and Supporting the Leadership of AANHPI Girls and Gender Expansive Youth* (2024), 9.

19. Ibid., 10.

20. Ibid., 24.

21. Southern Black Girls and Women's Consortium, https://www.southernblackgirls.org/our-work/.

22. Wheelock genealogy, biography of Lucy Wheelock (1857–1946), https://www.wheelockgenealogy.com/pages/lucywbio.htm.

23. K. Stringer, "No One Would Hire Her. So She Wrote Title IX and Changed History for Millions of Women. Meet Education Trailblazer Patsy Mink," The74million.org, https://www.the74million.org/article/no-one-would-hire-her-so-she-wrote-title-ix-and-changed-history-for-millions-of-women-meet-education-trailblazer-patsy-mink/.

24. Statista.com, "Number of Girls Participating in High School Sports in the United States from 2012–13 to 2023–24," https://www.statista.com/statistics/197591/female-participation-in-us-high-school-athletic-programs.

25. LeanInGirls.org, https://www.leaningirls.org.

26. Adam Grant. "Why Girls Get Called Bossy, and How to Avoid It," *Psychology Today,* https://www.psychologytoday.com/us/blog/give-and-take/201403/why-girls-get-called-bossy-and-how-to-avoid-it.

27. See womensagenda.com, "Your Daughter Isn't Bossy, She Has 'Executive Leadership Skills': Lessons from Sheryl Sandberg," https://womensagenda.com.au/latest/your-daughter-isn-t-bossy-she-has-executive-leadership-skills-lessons-from-sheryl-sandberg.

28. Black Lives Matter, or BLM, is a social movement that formed in response to the rise of state violence against Black people in the United States. The movement affirms that the lives of Black people are valuable and rejects the treatment of people of African descent as disposable.

29. J. Calvert and V. Asanovic, *Teen Trailblazers: 30 Fearless Girls Who Changed the World Before They Were 20* (Castle Point Books, 2018).

30. Frank Deford, "Mrs. Billie Jean King!" *Sports Illustrated* (May 19, 1975), https://vault.si.com/vault/1975/05/19/mrs-billie-jean-king.

31. The "Battle of the Sexes" tennis match was held on September 20, 1973, in Houston, Texas. Billie Jean King played against John Riggs in a televised match to challenge the notion that women were inferior athletes. Riggs, claiming that women's sports were so inferior that even an aged male player could beat the best female player, was defeated by King in straight sets, 6–4, 6–3, 6–3. The match—and Billie Jean King's win—is credited with igniting a boom in female sports participation. See: https://www.billiejeanking.com/battle-of-the-sexes.

32. Elizabeth Alexander, "The Trayvon Generation: For Solo, Simon, Robel, Maurice, and Sekou," *The New Yorker* (June 15, 2020), https://www.newyorker.com/magazine/2020/06/22/the-trayvon-generation.

33. The term "Black girl magic," a phrase coined by CaShawn Thomas in 2013, celebrates the mystifying innovation, beauty, and resilience of Black women and girls. The term was first used and popularized on the social media platform formerly known as Twitter.

34. Alexander, "The Trayvon Generation."

35. Joanna Stern, "They Used Smartphone Cameras to Record Police Brutality—and Change History: Video-camera Technology on Our Phones Got Better. In the Process, It Made Eyewitnesses of Us All," *Wall Street Journal* (June 13, 2020), https://www.wsj.com/articles/they-used-smartphone-cameras-to-record-police-brutalityand-change-history-11592020827.

36. Malala Yousafzai is an advocate for girls' access to education. While her work began as a young advocate in Pakistan, it has grown to global significance. Learn more at https://malala.org/.

37. Adverse Childhood Experiences (ACEs) refer to childhood traumas as measured by a survey that documents exposure to a host of harms that occur before the age of eighteen. See MT Baglivio et al. "The Relationship Between Adverse Childhood Experiences (ACE) and Juvenile Offending Trajectories in a Juvenile Offender Sample," *Journal of Criminal Justice* (2015).

38. A Long Walk Home. See https://alongwalkhome.org.

39. Latinas y Lideres. See https://www.latinaslideres.com.

40. Justice for Black Girls. See https://www.justiceforblackgirls.com.

2. Elevate Purpose over Punishment

1. The Nancy Drew mystery series is a collection of 175 novels and thirty-four revised stories written under the pseudonym Carolyn Keene and published by various companies since 1930. The stories center on a fictional teenage sleuth named Nancy Drew, who solves mysteries alone or in partnership with others. *Ramona the Pest* by Beverly Cleary is the lead book of a series that centers on the various adventures of the fictional character Ramona Quimby. Judy Blume is an American author of children's, young adult, and adult fiction. I began with *Tales of a Fourth Grade Nothing* (1972), and included *Are You There God? It's Me, Margaret* (1970), *Blubber* (1974), and others.

2. *Jubilee* (1966) by Margaret Walker is the story of a biracial girl enslaved in the American South. It is a semifictional, historical novel that introduced me to the violence of slavery from the perspective of a girl who is the product of the enslaved and the enslaver. Maya Angelou's *I Know Why the Caged Bird Sings* (1969) is an autobiographical text that chronicles her young life across the United States, including her time spent in San Francisco. *The Bluest Eye* (1970) by Toni Morrison tells the story of a young girl in Ohio who is reconciling her own identity through the gaze of white standards of beauty, excellence, and belonging.

3. St. Dominic's Catholic Church is a parish established in 1873, located in the section of San Francisco historically referred to as the Western Edition or Fillmore District. Finished in 1928, the church is both an active place of worship and a tourist interest for its architecture.

4. Parentification is when a child is thrust into taking on the responsibilities of an adult in the household. Parentified children often have caregiving responsibilities, as well as financial and/or other developmentally inappropriate roles within the family. See *Psychology Today*, https://www.psychologytoday.com/us/basics/parentification.

5. Adultification is the practice of interpreting the behaviors of girls as more adult-like. It is an age compression that produces bias and distorts an adult's perception of the actions taken by a biological child. Girls who are adultified are viewed as being in need of less protection, nurturing, and comfort. See Georgetown Center for Gender Justice and Opportunity, https://genderjusticeandopportunity.georgetown.edu/focus-areas/adultification-bias.

6. Summerbrige San Francisco, now called the Breakthrough Summerbridge, was founded in 1978 by the leadership and faculty of San Francisco University High School. Breakthrough Summerbridge is an award-winning, tuition-free, year-round and summer intensive academic enrichment and advocacy program. See https://www.sfuhs.org/summerbridge.

7. REACH4INFORMATION. See https://reachus.org/sexual-violence-info.

8. Malidoma Patrice Some, *The Healing Wisdom of Africa: Finding Life Purpose Through Nature, Ritual, and Community,* (New York: Jeremy Tarcher/Putnam, 1998), 33.

9. Ibid., 36.

10. The documentary is based on two of my books—*Pushout: The Criminalization of Black Girls in Schools* and *Sing a Rhythm, Dance a Blues: Education for the Liberation of Black and Brown Girls.* The film, produced by Women in the Room Productions, aired on PBS in 2019.

11. J. He, X. Yan, R.Wang, et al., "Does Childhood Adversity Lead to Drug Addiction in Adulthood? A Study of Serial Mediators Based on Resilience and Depression," *Front Psychiatry* 13:871459 (April 18, 2022), 10.3389/fpsyt.2022.871459. PMID: 35509889; PMCID: PMC9058108.l.

12. Monique W. Morris (Couvson), "Why Black Girls Are Targeted for Punishment in School—And How to Change That," TED Women, 2018.

13. Alliance for Girls, KPIX [video], *Sexual Harassment: Oakland Unified Schools Considers Changes to Its Sexual Harassment Policy,* 2017, https://www.alliance4girls.org/blog/press/beyond-anger-working-together-to-end-colonial-day-slap-ss-fridays-and-colonial-mentalities-in-oakland.

14. "Unchained at Last: Child Marriage in the U.S.," https://www.unchainedatlast.org/child-marriage-in-the-u-s.

15. Ibid.

16. S. Misra, EqualityNow.org, "Why Women's Rights Are Vulnerable in America" (March 8, 2024), https://equalitynow.org/news_and_insights/why-womens-rights-are-vulnerable-in-america.

17. See Sharita Forrest, "A Sense of Purpose May Have Significant Impact on Teens' Emotional Wellbeing," University of Illinois, Champaign-Urbana (February 13, 2023), https://news.illinois.edu/view/6367/230263956.

18. Ayse Yemiscigil, Melis Sena Yilmaz, and Matthew T. Lee, "How to Find Your Purpose," *Harvard Business Review* (September 15, 2023), https://hbr.org/2023/09/how-to-find-your-purpose.

19. Self-regulation refers to the ability to control one's own ideas and actions, without the intervention or guidance of others. According to Stosny, behavioral self-regulation refers to "the ability to act in your long-term best interest, consistent with your deepest values." See Steven Stosny, "Self-Regulation," *Psychology Today,* https://www.psychologytoday.com/us/blog/anger-in-the-age-entitlement/201110/self-regulation.

20. Equal Justice Society, https://equaljusticesociety.org.

21. Manning Marable, *How Capitalism Underdeveloped Black America: Problems in Race, Political Economy and Society* (Boston: South End Press, 1983), 158.

3. Dismantle the Structural Barriers to Her Success

1. Violations of the law that are associated with a person's ability to meet basic needs during a period of financial scarcity or hardship are called "survival crimes." These include: vagrancy, driving without a license, panhandling, illicit commercial sex work, and other offenses.

2. Project 2025, a presidential transition project, is the controversial conservative political agenda of President Donald Trump. The document is intended to "build on four pillars that will, collectively, pave the way for an effective conservative administration: a policy agenda, personnel, training, and a 180-day playbook." See https://www.project2025.org/about/about-project-2025. See also C. Contorno and C. Tolan, "Trump Said He Hadn't Read Project 2025—But Most of His Early Executive Actions Overlap with Its Proposals," CNN.com (January 31, 2025), https://www.cnn.com/2025/01/31/politics/trump-policy-project-2025-executive-orders-invs/index.html.

3. A. Gomez Licon, "Trump Was Challenged after Blaming DEI for the DC Plane Crash. Here's What He Said," Associated Press (January 30, 2025), https://apnews.com/article/plane-crash-washington-dc-trump-dei-claims-3ac5486ec594d81e919e8ebbd9733869.

4. Proposition 209, of the California Civil Rights Initiative, was a ballot initiative passed in 1996 which banned the consideration of race, sex, gender identity, ethnicity, color, or national origin in decisions made in public education, contracting, and employment. Its amendment to the state constitution to "prohibit discrimination on based on race, sex, color, ethnicity or national education" eliminated race- and gender-based affirmative action to respond to decades of discrimination against people of color and women of all racial groups in the public sector.

5. Thelton E. Henderson Center for Social Justice. UC Berkeley Law School. Available at https://www.law.berkeley.edu/wp-content/uploads/2016/07/A_Higher_Hurdle_December_2008.pdf.

6. All of Us or None, https://prisonerswithchildren.org/all-of-us-or-none.

7. National Associations of Commissions for Women, https://www.nacw.org.

8. The White House, Obama White House Archives, https://obamawhitehouse.archives.gov/administration/eop/cwg.

9. The White House Gender Policy Council, https://www.whitehouse.gov/gpc.

10. The White House, National Strategy on Gender Equity and Equality (2021), https://www.whitehouse.gov/wp-content/uploads/2021/10/National-Strategy-on-Gender-Equity-and-Equality.pdf.

11. Philadelphia Commission for Women, Annual Report (2019), 13, https://www.phila.gov/media/20200313191747/2019-womens-commission-annual-report.pdf.

12. Girls for Gender Equity, www.ggenyc.org.

13. Girls for Gender Equity, *Breaking Silence: A Hearing on Girls of Color* (NYC) video, https://www.youtube.com/watch?v=QqD7r1bkK4Y

14. Girls for Gender Equity, "Annual Report and Recommendations," February 2022, https://ggenyc.org/annual-report/ywi-report-and-recommendations/.

15. Girls for Gender Equity, https://ggenyc.org/wp-content/uploads/2017/11/GGE_school_girls_deserveDRAFT6FINALWEB.pdf.

16. Grace Sato, "Quantifying Hope 2017: Philanthropic Support for Black Men and Boys," The Foundation Center and the Campaign for Black Male Achievement, https://www.issuelab.org/resources/28352/28352.pdf.

17. Urban Institute, "New York City's Young Men's Initiative" (January 2016), https://www.urban.org/sites/default/files/publication/75996/2000533-New-York-Citys-Young-Mens-Initiative-Status-Report-and-Future-Directions.pdf.

18. California Funders for Men and Boys of Color, "Celebrating Five Years of Collective Action" (2019), https://cafundersforbmoc.org/wp-content/uploads/2019/12/CFBMoC-Anniversary-2019-r5-reader-spreads-1.pdf.

19. Ibid.

20. Girls for Gender Equity, "Programs: Sisters in Strength," https://ggenyc.org/programs/#:~:text=Sisters%20In%20Strength%20(SIS)&text=GGE%20served%20as%20the%20fiscal,violence%2C%20and%20child%20sexual%20assault.

21. D.L. Cooperrider and S. Srivastva, "Appreciative Inquiry In Organizational Life (1987)". In R.W. Woodman and W.A. Pasmore (Eds.), *Research in Organizational Change and Development*, 129–169. Stamford, CT: JAI Press.

22. Lucille Clifton, "homage to my hips," from *Good Woman* (Curtis Brown, 1987), https://www.poetryfoundation.org/poems/49487/homage-to-my-hips.

4. Protect Girls from Gender-Based Violence

1. Rosario Dawson, Twitter @rosariodawson (October 15, 2017).

2. Tarana Burke, *Unbound: My Story of Liberation and the Birth of the Me Too Movement* (New York: Flatiron Books, Asantewaa Group, 2021).

3. Factored into this analysis are medical costs, loss of work productivity among

survivors and perpetrators, activities related to the criminal legal system, and victim property loss or damage. See Cora Peterson, Sarah DeGue, Curtis Florence, and Colby Lokey, *Lifetime Economic Burden of Rape Among U.S. Adults,* Centers for Disease Control (n.d.), https://pubmed.ncbi.nlm.nih.gov/28153649.

4. E. J. Letourneau, T. W. M. Roberts, L. Malone, and Y. Sun, "No Check We Won't Write: A Report on the High Cost of Sex Offender Incarceration," *Sexual Abuse* 35, no. 1 (2023), 54–82, https://doi.org/10.1177/10790632221078305.

5. Ibid.

6. Ibid. See also https://magazine.publichealth.jhu.edu/2022/stopping-child-sexual-abuse-requires-shift-funding-priorities.

7. D. Finkelhor, H. Turner, D. Colburn, "The Prevalence of Child Sexual with Online Abuse Added," *Child Abuse & Neglect* 149 (2024), https://www.unh.edu/ccrc/sites/default/files/media/2024-02/finkelhor-ocsa-csa-24.pdf.

8. Berkeley Media Studies Group, *Case by Case: News Coverage of Child Sexual Abuse 2007–2009* (2011), https://www.bmsg.org/wp-content/uploads/2011/05/bmsg_issue19.pdf.

9. Ibid., 7.

10. United Nations Human Rights Council, "Study on the Sexual Abuse and Exploitation of Children in the Entertainment Industry: Report of the Special Rapporteur on the Sale, Sexual Exploitation and Sexual Abuse of Children," Mama Fatima Singhateh (2024), https://documents.un.org/doc/undoc/gen/g23/266/75/pdf/g2326675.pdf.

11. Office on Women's Health in the U.S. Department of Health and Human Services, "Disparities and the Leading Causes of Death in Women—National Women's Health Week" (2023).

12. *A Different World* was a popular sitcom in the United States, which aired for six seasons between 1987 and 1993. Created by Bill Cosby, the show is a spin-off of *The Cosby Show,* and follows the life of students who attend a fictional Historically Black College, Hillman College. *Grey's Anatomy,* created by Shonda Rhimes, is an American medical drama that launched in 2005 and focuses on the personal and professional lives of young doctors at the fictional Grey Sloan Memorial Hospital.

13. The five provisions in question were: "1) doctors were required to inform women considering abortion about its potential negative impacts on their health; 2) women were required to give notice to husbands before obtaining an abortion; 3) children were required to get consent from a parent or guardian; 4) a 24-hour waiting period was required between deciding to have an abortion and undergoing

the procedure; and 5) reporting requirements were imposed on facilities offering abortions." See *Planned Parenthood of Southeastern PA v. Casey,* 505 U.S. 833 (1992).

14. Wallace Terry, *Bloods: Black Veterans of the Vietnam War: An Oral History* (Presidio Press, 1985).

15. World Bank, "Violence Against Women and Girls—What the Data Tell Us" (October 1, 2022), https://genderdata.worldbank.org/en/data-stories/overview-of-gender-based-violence.

16. UN Women, "Facts and Figures: Ending Violence Against Women" (November 25, 2024), https://www.unwomen.org/en/what-we-do/ending-violence-against-women/facts-and-figures#_ednref9.

17. UNICEF, "A Familiar Face: Violence in the Lives of Children and Adolescents" (November 1, 2017), https://data.unicef.org/resources/a-familiar-face.

18. World Health Organization, "Violence Against Women" (March 25, 2024), https://www.who.int/news-room/fact-sheets/detail/violence-against-women.

19. World Economic Forum, "To Takle Violence Against Women, We Need to Alleviate Poverty" (November 3, 2022), https://www.weforum.org/stories/2022/11/to-take-violence-against-women-alleviate-poverty/#:~:text=Poverty%20increases%20women's%20vulnerability%20to,exploitation%20such%20as%20human%20trafficking.

20. U.S. Department of Labor, https://www.dol.gov/sites/dolgov/files/ODEP/pdf/Spotlight-on-Women-with-Disabilities-March-2021.pdf.

21. J. C. Campbell, "Health Consequences of Intimate Partner Violence," *Lancet* 359, no. 9314 (April 13, 2002): 1331–36, doi: 10.1016/S0140-6736(02)08336-8; PMID: 11965295.

22. Agenda Alliance, "Women's Mental Health Facts," https://www.agendaalliance.org/our-work/projects-and-campaigns/womens-mental-health-facts/#:~:text=Mental%20ill%20health%20among%20young,fifth%20most%20common%20for%20boys.

23. E. M. Gaylor, K. H. Krause, L. E. Welder, et al., "Suicidal Thoughts and Behaviors Among High School Students—Youth Risk Behavior Survey, United States, 2021," *MMWR* 72, Suppl 1 (2023): 45–54, http://dx.doi.org/10.15585/mmwr.su7201a6.

24. A. R. Flores, B. D. M. Wilson, L. L. Langton, and I. H. Meyer, "Victimization at the Intersections of Sexual Orientation, Gender Identity, and Race: National Crime Victimization Survey, 2017–2019," *PLoS One* 18, no. 2 (February 9, 2023), e0281641. doi: 10.1371/journal.pone.0281641. PMID: 36758033; PMCID: PMC9910698.

25. Michael T. Baglivio, Kevin T. Wolff, Alex R. Piquero, and Nathan Epps, "The Relationship Between Adverse Childhood Experiences (ACE) and Juvenile Offending Trajectories in a Juvenile Offender Sample," *Journal of Criminal Justice* 43, no. 3 (2015): 229–41, ISSN 0047-2352, https://doi.org/10.1016/j.jcrimjus.2015.04.012.

26. Melissa S. Jones, Hayley Pierce, and Kevin Shafer, "Gender Differences in Early Adverse Childhood Experiences and Youth Psychological Distress," *Journal of Criminal Justice* 83 (2022), 101925, ISSN 0047-2352; https://doi.org/10.1016/j.jcrimjus.2022.101925.

27. Integrative Life Center, "What Are the Long-Term Effects of Childhood Trauma?" (August 3, 2021), https://integrativelifecenter.com/mental-health-treatment/what-are-the-long-term-effects-of-childhood-trauma/#:~:text=The%20emotional%20and%20psychological%20damage,Suicidal%20ideation.

28. Ibid.

29. G. Martinez and K. Daniels, "Fertility of Men and Women Aged 15–49 in the United States: National Survey of Family Growth, 2015–2019," U.S. Department of Health and Human Services, Centers for Disease Control and Prevention (January 10, 2023), https://www.cdc.gov/nchs/data/nhsr/nhsr179.pdf.

30. A. Radford, E. Toombs, K. Zugic, et al., "Examining Adverse Childhood Experiences (ACEs) Within Indigenous Populations: A Systematic Review," *J Child Adolesc Trauma* 15, no. 2 (August 18, 2021): 401–21, doi: 10.1007/s40653-021-00393-7; PMID: 35600513; PMCID: PMC9120316. See also J. M. Craig et al., "All in the Family? Exploring the Intergenerational Transmission of Exposure of Adverse Childhood Experiences and Their Effect on Offending Behavior," *Youth Violence and Juvenile Justice* (2021).

31. Z. Giano, R. L. Camplain, C. Camplain, et al., "Adverse Childhood Events in American Indian/Alaska Native Populations," *American Journal of Preventive Medicine* 60, no. 2 (2021): 213–21, https://doi.org/10.1016/j.amepre.2020.08.020.

32. Ibid.

33. The Red Road, https://theredroad.org/issues/missing-murdered-indigenous-women.

34. Urban Indian Health Institute, "Missing and Murdered Indigenous Women and Girls: A Snapshot of Data from 71 Urban Cities in the United States," https://www.uihi.org/wp-content/uploads/2018/11/Missing-and-Murdered-Indigenous-Women-and-Girls-Report.pdf.

35. Linda A. Seabrook, "Shining a Light on the Crisis of Missing or Murdered Black Women and Girls in the United States," U.S. Department of Justice, Office

of Justice Programs, https://www.ojp.gov/safe-communities/inside-perspectives/shining-light-on-the-crisis-of-missing-or-murdered-black-women-and-girls-in-the-united-states.

36. A Long Walk Home, https://alongwalkhome.org/about-us.

37. Statista, "Share of Adults Aged 18–64 Years Without Health Insurance in the United States from 2015 to 2023, by Gender," https://www.statista.com/statistics/1276674/percentage-of-us-adults-without-health-insurance-by-gender. See also KFF, Women's Health Insurance Coverage, https://www.kff.org/womens-health-policy/fact-sheet/womens-health-insurance-coverage/.

38. L. Overhage, R. Hailu, A. B. Busch, et al., "Trends in Acute Care Use for Mental Health Conditions Among Youth During the COVID-19 Pandemic," *JAMA Psychiatry* 80, no. 9 (2023): 924–32. doi:10.1001/jamapsychiatry.2023.2195. https://jamanetwork.com/journals/jamapsychiatry/fullarticle/2806889.

39. Nadine Burke Harris, *The Deepest Well: Healing the Long-Term Effects of Childhood Trauma and Adversity* (New York: Mariner Books, 2018), 41.

40. World Food Program, "Women Are Hungrier" (n.d.), https://www.wfpusa.org/women-are-hungrier-infographic.

41. Feeding America's Children, Feedingac.org. See https://www.feedingac.org.

42. NoKidHungry.org, "Facts About Child Hunger in America" (2022). See https://www.nokidhungry.org/who-we-are/hunger-facts.

43. MoveforHunger.org, "Why Women Are Facing Hunger at a Disproportionate Rate" (2025). See: https://moveforhunger.org/how-hunger-disproportionately-affects-women.

44. K. Travis, "Facing Hunger at Inordinate Rates: Women and the Food Insecurity Act," American Medical Women's Association, AMWA.org, https://www.amwa-doc.org/facing-hunger-at-inordinate-rates-women-and-the-food-insecurity-act/#:~:text=Women's%20experiences%20with%20food%20insecurity,in%20respect%20to%20prenatal%20health.

45. Allison Torres Burtka, Global Sport Matters, Arizona State University, "Understanding the Barriers that Get in the way of Latina Girls Playing Sports," https://live-global-sport-matter.ws.asu.edu/research/2020/11/17/understanding-the-barriers-that-get-in-the-way-of-latina-girls-playing-sports/.

46. N. Zarrett and P. T. Veliz, "The Healing Power of Sport: COVID-19 and Girls' Participation, Health, and Achievement," Women's Sports Foundation (2023), https://www.womenssportsfoundation.org/wp-content/uploads/2023/01/The-Healing-Power-of-Sport-FINAL.pdf.

5. Invest in Girls' Education and Mentorship

1. National Black Women's Justice Institute, Black Girls' Pushout and Criminalization in Schools Data Hub (2024). The U.S. Department of Education's Civil Rights Data Collection (CRDC) data are analyzed for the 2011–18 academic years. See https://www.nbwji.org/school-pushout-data.

2. Ibid.

3. Ibid.

4. U.S. Government Accountability Office, "K–12 Education: Nationally Black Girls Receive More Frequent and More Severe Discipline in School than Other Girls" (September 2024), https://www.gao.gov/assets/gao-24-106787.pdf.

5. Ibid.

6. See Danielle Smith, Nickolaus A. Ortiz, Jamilia J. Blake, et al., "Tipping Point: Effect of the Number of In-school Suspensions on Academic Failure," *Contemporary School Psychology* 25 (December 2021): 466–75.

7. Gwen's Girls, Pittsburgh, PA, https://gwensgirls.org/home.

8. Monique Couvson (Morris), *Sing a Rhythm, Dance a Blues: Liberatory Education for Black and Brown Girls* (New York: The New Press, 2019), 8.

9. Ibid.

10. Bessel van der Kolk, *The Body Keeps the Score: Brain, Mind, and Body in the Healing of Trauma* (New York: Penguin Books, 2014).

11. Ibid.

12. The Sanctuary Institute, "The Sanctuary Model," https://www.thesanctuaryinstitute.org/about-us/the-sanctuary-model.

13. Ibid.

14. Ibid.

15. Gwen's Girls, "Gwen's Girls Takes Restorative Approach to Help Girls Heal from Trauma" (August 14, 2019), https://gwensgirls.org/gwens-girls-takes-restorative-approach-to-help-girls-heal-from-trauma.

16. See Monique Couvson (Morris), *Pushout: The Criminalization of Black Girls in Schools* (New York: The New Press, 2016); *Sing a Rhythm, Dance a Blues*; and *Cultivating Joyful Learning Spaces for Black Girls: Insights into Interrupting School Pushout* (ASCD, 2022).

17. Congress.gov, https://www.congress.gov/bill/118th-congress/house-bill/2690.

18. U.S. Government Accountability Office, "K–12 Education."

19. Ibid.

20. Ayanna Pressley. X.com @AyannaPressley. https://x.com/AyannaPressley/status/1740424875225788557?mx=2.

21. The CROWN Act, created in 2019 by Dove and the CROWN (Creating a Respectful and Open World for Natural Hair) Coalition, in partnership with then–State Senator Holly J. Mitchell of California, is legislation to "ensure protection against discrimination based on race-based hairstyles by extending statutory protection to hair texture and protective styles such as braids, locs, twists, and knots in the workplace and public schools." See https://www.thecrownact.com.

22. Representative Ayanna Pressley, *Reps. Pressley, Pelosi, DeLauro Unveil Groundbreaking Report on Pushout of Black Girls in Schools* [video], https://www.youtube.com/watch?v=OvNPnj0Lg68.

23. Center for American Women and Politics, "Women Serving in the 199th Congress, 2025–2027" (2025), https://cawp.rutgers.edu/facts/levels-office/congress/women-serving-119th-congress-2025-2027.

24. Aileen C. Hernandez. "Racism and Sexism Must Be Vanquished," in Mary Ellen Butler, ed., *Black Women Stirring the Waters* (Marcus Books Printing, 1997), xi.

25. Hernandez, "Racism and Sexism Must Be Vanquished," 73.

26. Ibid.

27. UN Women, "Facts & Figures: Poverty and Hunger," https://www.unwomen.org/en/news/in-focus/commission-on-the-status-of-women-2012/facts-and-figures#:~:text=fare%20much%20better.-,Education,urban%20boys%20(60%20percent).

28. U.S. Department of State, "Girls' Education." See https://2009-2017.state.gov/s/gwi/c62293.htm.

29. Institute for Women's Policy Research, "Poverty, Gender, and Public Policies" (February 2016), https://iwpr.org/wp-content/uploads/2020/08/D505-Poverty-Gender-and-Public-Policies.pdf#:~:text=Just%20over%2016%20percent%20of%20women%20and%20girls,13.4%20percent%20of%20the%20male%20population%20%28Figure%201%29.

30. J. Cheeseman Day and C. Christnacht, "Women Hold 76% of All Health Care Jobs, Gaining in Higher-Paying Occupations" (August 14, 2019), https://www.census.gov/library/stories/2019/08/your-health-care-in-womens-hands.html.

31. Development Dimensions International, "Women as Mentors: Does She or Doesn't She?; A Global Study of Business Women and Mentoring" (2013), https://media.ddiworld.com/research/women-as-mentors_research_ddi.pdf.

32. Massachusetts Institute of Technology, "The Gender Gap in STEM: Still Gaping in 2023," https://professionalprograms.mit.edu/blog/leadership/the-gender-gap-in-stem/#:~:text=The%20gender%20gap%20in%20STEM%20has%20

been%20attributed%20to%20several,pursuing%20STEM%20education%20and%20careers.

33. T. Yogurtcu, "The Role of STEM Education in Achieving Gender Equality," Forbes.com (May 20, 2022), https://www.forbes.com/sites/forbestechcouncil/2022/05/20/the-role-of-stem-education-in-achieving-gender-equality.

34. Center for American Women and Politics, "Women Serving in the 199th Congress, 2025–2027."

35. Represent Women, "2023 Gender Parity Index: The Status of Women's Representation in 2023," https://www.representwomen.org/2022_gender_parity_index.

36. Changing Perspectives, "5 Core Competencies of Social-Emotional Learning Fundamentals," https://changingperspectivesnow.org/2024/04/11/5-core-competencies-of-social-emotional-learning-fundamentals/#:~:text=The%20Five%20Core%20Competencies%20of%20SEL&text=These%20competencies%20are%20self%2Dawareness,look%20at%20each%20of%20them.

37. The White House, "My Brother's Keeper 2016 Progress Report: Two Years of Expanding Opportunity and Creating Pathways to Success" (2016), https://obamawhitehouse.archives.gov/sites/whitehouse.gov/files/images/MBK-2016-Progress-Report.pdf.

38. Dana Brownlee, "Career Mentorship Stops Confidence Slide for Teen Girls, Study Finds," Forbes.com (January 11, 2023), https://www.forbes.com/sites/danabrownlee/2023/01/11/career-mentorship-stops-confidence-slide-for-teen-girls-study-finds.

39. Ibid.

40. National Black Women's Justice Institute, www.nbwji.org.

6. Make the Financial Investment

1. T. Jan, J. McGregor, and M. Hoyer, "Corporate America's $50 Billion Promise," *Washington Post* (August 23, 2001), https://www.washingtonpost.com/business/interactive/2021/george-floyd-corporate-america-racial-justice. See also K. Baskin, "What Corporate Philanthropy Got Wrong after George Floyd's Murder," MIT Management Sloan School (March 16, 2022), https://mitsloan.mit.edu/ideas-made-to-matter/what-corporate-philanthropy-got-wrong-after-george-floyds-murder#:~:text=For%20example%2C%20Google%20committed%20to,to%20Black%20and%20Latino%20communities.

2. See SecondMuse Capital, https://www.secondmusecapital.com.

3. SecondMuse Capital and Grantmakers for Girls of Color (G4GC), "Abundantly Investing in Girls, Femmes, and Gender Expansive Youth of Color:

Summary of Findings" (2022), Montreal, Quebec, Canada and Brooklyn, NY, https://www.secondmusecapital.com/_files/ugd/7e7cc4_6612db4acd4b4ab7bf94edd4cf7b56a1.pdf. See Appendix B for the full list of the eighteen catalytic factors.

4. Ibid.

5. Supreme Court of the United States, *Dobbs, State Health Officer of The Mississippi Department of Health et al. v. Jackson Women's Health Organization et al.* (2021), https://www.supremecourt.gov/opinions/21pdf/19-1392_6j37.pdf.

6. Centers for Disease Control and Prevention, "Youth Risk Behavior Survey Data Summary & Trends Report: 2013–2023," U.S. Department of Health and Human Services (2024), https://www.cdc.gov/yrbs/dstr/pdf/YRBS_Data-Summary-Trends_Report2023_508.pdf. See also NBC News.com, https://www.nbcnews.com/health/health-news/cdc-sexual-attacks-teen-girls-increased-lockdown-rcna70782.

7. Karen Zraick, "Man Charged with Hate Crimes After 7 Asian Women Are attacked in 2 Hours," *New York Times* (March 2, 2022).

8. Supreme Court of the United States, *Students for Fair Admissions, Inc. v. President and Fellows of Harvard College* (2022), https://www.supremecourt.gov/opinions/22pdf/20-1199_hgdj.pdf.

9. Ibid.

10. Ibid.

11. Annie E. Casey Foundation Data Center (updated July 2024), https://datacenter.aecf.org/data/tables/103-child-population-by-race-and-ethnicity#detailed/1/any/false/2545,1095,2048,574,1729,37,871,870,573,869/72,66,67,8367,69,70,71,12/423,424.

12. Statista.com, "Number of Bachelor's Degrees Earned in the United States from 1949/50 to 2031/32, by Gender," https://www.statista.com/statistics/185157/number-of-bachelor-degrees-by-gender-since-1950/.

13. Liam Knox, "An Early Look at Diversity Post-Affirmative Action," Inside Higher Ed. (September 6, 2023), https://www.insidehighered.com/news/admissions/traditional-age/2024/09/06/early-look-racial-diversity-post-affirmative-action.

14. A. Kaiyo, M. Grande, K. Artwell Murapa, and M. Napthali Mupa, "Unmet Standards for Diversity, Equity, and Inclusion (DEI) in the USA & Recommendations to Meet the Standards," *IRE Journals* 8, no. 4 (October 2024), https://www.irejournals.com/formatedpaper/1706444.pdf.

15. D. Weissner, "Republican State Officials Threaten Legal Action over

Company Diversity Policies," Reuters.com (July 14, 2023), https://www.reuters.com/world/us/republican-state-officials-threaten-legal-action-over-company-diversity-policies-2023-07-13.

16. See https://www.insidehighered.com/news/quick-takes/2024/09/12/nc-universities-cut-59-positions-after-dei-policy-repeal#:~:text=North%20Carolina's%20four%2Dyear%20public,summary%20from%20the%20UNC%20system. See also https://www.washingtonpost.com/business/2024/06/27/conservative-lawsuits-topple-affirmative-action-dei.

17. Melinda French Gates, Pivotal Ventures, https://www.pivotalventures.org/articles/melinda-french-gates-announces-1billlion-commitment-to-advance-women-globally#:~:text=Melinda%20French%20Gates%20Announces%20$1B%20Commitment%20to%20Advance%20Women's%20Power%20Globally,-May%2028%2C%202024&text=Melinda%20French%20Gates%20announced%20that,women's%20power%20and%20influence%20globally.&text=With%20the%20ongoing%20rollback%20of,barriers%20that%20hold%20them%20back.

18. Cheryl Contee, "The Great Wealth Transfer: An $84 Trillion Investment Opportunity for Women," Forbes.com (November 18, 2024), https://www.forbes.com/councils/forbesbusinesscouncil/2024/11/18/the-great-wealth-transfer-an-84-trillion-investment-opportunity-for-women/#:~:text=By%202030%2C%20women%20are%20expected,divorce%20is%20also%20a%20factor.

19. *Oxford English Dictionary,* "Philanthropy."

20. Ms. Foundation for Women, "Pocket Change: How Women and Girls of Color Do More with Less" (July 1, 2020), https://forwomen.org/resources/pocket-change-report.

21. Trust-based Philanthropy, https://www.trustbasedphilanthropy.org/.

22. Our Collective Practice, https://www.ourcollectivepractice.org/about.

ABOUT THE AUTHOR

Monique Couvson, Ed.D. (formerly Monique W. Morris), president/CEO of G4GC and cofounder of the National Black Women's Justice Institute, is the author of several books, including *Pushout*; *Black Stats*; *Sing a Rhythm, Dance a Blues*; *Charisma's Turn*, and *Girls, Unlimited* (all from The New Press). Her work has been featured by *Time*, NPR, *The New York Times*, MSNBC, *Essence*, *The Atlantic*, TED, *The Washington Post*, *Education Week*, and others.

PUBLISHING IN THE PUBLIC INTEREST

Thank you for reading this book published by The New Press; we hope you enjoyed it. New Press books and authors play a crucial role in sparking conversations about the key political and social issues of our day.

We hope that you will stay in touch with us. To keep up to date with our books, events, and the issues we cover, follow us on social media and sign up for our newsletter at thenewpress.org.

Please consider buying New Press books not only for yourself, but also for friends and family and to donate to schools, libraries, community centers, prison libraries, and other organizations involved with the issues our authors write about.

The New Press is a 501(c)(3) nonprofit organization; if you wish to support our work with a tax-deductible gift please visit https://thenewpress.org/donate/ or use the QR code below.